grill
stylish food to sizzle

grill
stylish food to sizzle

Linda Tubby

with photographs by Martin Brigdale

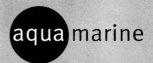

aquamarine

To Lou, Charlie, Tilly and Jack
where the love started

contents

introduction

There is, without a doubt, something very relaxing and pleasurable about cooking and eating grilled food.

Perhaps it is because cooking over coals is such a simple method of preparing food that even the most reluctant of family members join in enthusiastically if asked to help light the fire or tend the food, or it may be because it doesn't take much more than some basic equipment and good ingredients to produce a really wonderful meal.

Whatever the reason, the delicious aromas wafting across the garden, food gently sizzling on the grill rack or griddle, and the prospect of tackling hot, smoky food with the fingers is something that appeals to young and old alike, friends and families, small and large groups.

Grilling has been a popular method of cooking ever since primitive people first discovered that meat turned and cooked over a hot fire was better than the raw stuff. It's not clear who first coined the word barbecue, though one possible explanation is that it came from *barbacoa*, a raised platform used for cooking, which greatly impressed Spanish invaders when they encountered it in the Caribbean in the 15th century. The *barbacoa* grill rack was made of green (new) wood, and was primarily used to cook and preserve meat by smoking. Another suggestion is that the word comes from the French *barbe en queue*, meaning "beard to tail", which described the goats roasted by French settlers in the American state of Florida.

From its origins as a simple and useful way to cook and preserve meat, grilling today is a sophisticated method of cooking that creates a cultural link between many cuisines around the world. It can be as simple as the clay braziers and open beach fires of Spain and Portugal that are used for grilling sardines fresh from the sea, to spectacular operations such as the famous *asados* of South America, which require considerable skill and involve roasting whole animals upright on rods over an open fire.

Australians use the barbecue with great creativity, using the fire and grill rack to roast, grill, smoke and steam their fresh ingredients in backyards, on balconies and at the beach. They are largely responsible for changing the emphasis of grilling from being a practical method of cooking to one that is a relaxing, pleasurable activity. This can also be seen in the United States, and particularly in the south western states, who are renowned for their boldly flavoured grilled steaks and ribs, often cooked on large rotating spits. These dishes reflect the eclectic tastes of the Californians who, in turn, have soaked up influences from nearby Mexico and even South-East Asia.

Grilling is to be found in the gastronomic street cultures of many peoples, in particular those of the Arabs and Muslims from Morocco and Turkey to India and beyond to South-East Asia. In north Africa, the vendors in the Arab souks cook kebabs on small punched tin braziers, filling the air with mouthwatering aromas. In parts of Greece the tradition of roasting pork over charcoal in local tavernas is still acted out

every Sunday. The fire is started in the early morning, and a whole pig is spit roasted over the embers. By lunchtime it will be done and placed outside in a glass case, ready to be cut up on the spot as people come and order pieces for picnics or an easy lunch at home. In Morocco and other neighbouring countries, the Arab *mechoui*, meaning grill, is used for festive occasions, and involves the slow roasting of a whole lamb.

On an even greater scale are communal cookouts in pits or trenches. Examples are the clambakes of New England, which involve cooking food on layers of seaweed laid on stones heated by a fire, and the elaborate *umu* as constructed by the Samoans of the South Pacific. In this case, the fire is built over volcanic river stones. Giant taro leaves are used to enclose the food, then when the embers burn down and the stones glow hot, the parcel is layered between more stones in an elaborate sandwich. The food is traditionally a rich assortment of starchy vegetables, seafood and meats. A *luau* – a combination of young taro leaves, onion and coconut cream, which is wrapped in banana and breadfruit leaves – is cooked on top of the *umu*. The cooking only takes about 40 minutes, unlike the four hours required for a Polynesian *hangi*, where the fire pit is very deep, and freshly picked flax is used for the layering.

This diversity of ingredients, techniques and equipment is one of the most exciting things about grilling, and has greatly influenced the selection of recipes in this book. At the same time, however, a real part of the appeal of grilling is its familiarity – many of us have happy childhood memories of family barbecues, and simple ingredients such as baked vegetables or sausages still have pride of place at many a barbecue. I grew up in a tiny hamlet in the north of England, and every November, warmly wrapped against the cold, we would stay outside well into the night for the bonfire celebration. My father would provide the wood, while the farmer next door supplied the amply-sized potatoes. We children would sit bedazzled by the flames, waiting for the exciting moment when the potatoes would go in. No foil, just straight into the ash, which was still dotted with a few red embers. It didn't seem to take long for these scalding hot delights to be placed in our mitten-covered hands with their soft, creamy and nutty filling.

These early memories have been followed by many years' grilling and barbecueing, and eating food from around the world. The recipes in this book draw on all those influences, and rely on good quality ingredients, some basic skills and a sense of creativity. In most cases, the food is simple to prepare and, once you've learnt the secrets of controlling the temperature of the griddle or coals, the cooking is easy too. Barbecues and griddles come in all sizes and shapes, and these recipes are designed for maximum flavour, visual appeal and ease of cooking. I hope you enjoy cooking and eating them as much as I have.

using this book

Whether you have a barbecue or a griddle, or both, you'll discover recipes here that will suit every occasion and need.

This book is designed to let you plan your meal as you wish, using either a barbecue or a griddle, or a mixture of the two. There are also a few recipes included that demand something a bit more unusual, such as baking directly in the ashes of a fire or cooking in a pit on the beach.

When planning a menu, consider the number of people involved, the location, and whether you want a number of dishes to be ready all at once or whether they can be eaten as they are cooked. It can be a good idea to prepare a griddle recipe to start with so that you can take advantage of the initial blast of heat from a barbecue. When the coals are cooler, you can then move to cooking directly on the grill rack.

When entertaining, no cook wants to box themselves away in their own kitchen, especially in the first half hour when guests arrive. One of the wonderful things about food destined for the barbecue or griddle is that so much of the work can be done in advance. The recipes in this book have been selected to give you greatest flexibility and the four chapters are divided according to the preparation time involved. To begin with are dishes that can be put together in the time it takes to ready the fire, with no more than 30 minutes preparation needed. Next are

recipes that need a little more thought, but are still relatively easy to get ready. The third chapter features ideas that do involve some forward planning, such as when ingredients need to be marinated overnight. At the end are recipes that do not necessarily take long to cook, but might involve more special ingredients or a different style of cooking.

One of the fun aspects of cooking is being able to adapt recipes, swapping ingredients if one isn't available. For example, if you are not able to find pandanus leaves for wrapping fish or sugar cane to use as skewers, then replace these with heavy duty tin foil and ordinary wooden skewers. Such changes will in no way affect the flavour of the final dish.

If an unexpected downpour threatens to ruin your meal, just head indoors. Many of the recipes in this book can be used on either the barbecue or griddle. You'll find that there won't be a great deal of difference in the timing and, when you cook indoors, you won't have to contend with variables such as wind direction.

A superb, relaxed meal is the goal of this book, not rigid perfection. One final word of advice: the open air, punctuated with delicious aromas, really does stimulate the appetite – so it's perhaps best to double up on quantities if you can.

There are days when spending a few hours preparing a meal is highly enjoyable, but at other times putting a meal together in minutes is what counts. Dishes don't need to be complicated: strawberry and marshmallow kebabs, top left, potato skewers with haloumi slices, centre, and even the humble sausage, top right, look good, smell great and taste superb when grilled.

barbecues and griddles

Think carefully about what you need before you spend a fortune on an impressive but rarely used barbecue.

You may find all you need is a small portable barbecue rather than a huge gas burner with a back-up kitchen attached. It is probably best to start small and enlarge as needed.

do-it-yourself grilling

Improvised grilling can be deeply satisfying. If it is the ritual that you enjoy, rather than the idea of getting a fire started quickly, then this is for you. All you need is a safe place where the fire can be contained for long enough to establish a base of hot embers, a source of fuel such as wood or charcoal, the means to ignite it, and a rack to cook on. A wood fire will take about 2 hours from building to being ready for cooking.

One step up from this is a kit for a built-in barbecue, which comes with its own tray and grill rack. Buying the bricks and building a permanent barbecue area is fun, but it is vital to think about the location before you begin. Avoid siting the barbecue too close to buildings, fences or trees.

choosing a barbecue

Visit any barbecue showroom and you will be amazed at the variety of grills on offer. Weighing up which one to buy is a very personal choice. Many prefer charcoal, largely because getting the hands dirty feels more fun, and it has the slight unpredictability of a real fire.

charcoal barbecues

There are three main categories of charcoal barbecue. The first is the portable type, which includes the original Japanese hibachis. Basically a firebox on tall or short legs, these have a tray in the base to hold the coals and there are several rungs for the grill rack so that the height can be varied, depending on the heat required. They also have a windshield at the back that becomes a lid for easy portability. Another portable type has a double non-adjustable grill rack in shiny tin, and can fold up, making it a great travelling barbecue.

The easiest of portable barbecues have to be disposable ones. They come with their own coals, set under a fixed fine-mesh grill rack, and have a fuel-soaked material pad on top of them for easy ignition. These disposable barbecues can be placed directly on the ground or sand, or on a table, in which case it is advisable to insulate the surface with a separate stand. When using this type, it is important to keep the food moving all the time, as the heat cannot be controlled, or choose something that cooks quickly and doesn't need turning.

The second category of charcoal grill is the brazier. These normally have an open firebox on a stand, with a windshield at the back, which is helpful when getting the fire started.

Before buying a barbecue, consider where you are most likely to use it, and the amount of food you will want to cook. Small portable grill racks and barbecues, top left and centre, are great for romantic getaways, while the kettle barbecue is an excellent family choice, top right.

9

Opposite, clockwise from top left: Buying a barbecue needn't be a formidable investment. They can be old or new, small or large, and can be anything from an old Afghan cooker, an Arabian punched-tin barbecue, a terracotta oven, to a shiny fold-out portable barbecue. There are also pot-bellied braziers, squat terracotta barbecues, and simple metal grill racks, above.

Another type of brazier is the pedestal barbecue. Made from shiny stainless steel, this looks very attractive but must be used carefully. The pedestal is tightly packed with balls of newspaper, which, when lit, ignite the coals on a rack above. The base gets very hot, so it is vital to place it on a level flameproof surface. This type of barbecue can also have a motor-driven spit attached.

A favourite barbecue in this category is the pot-bellied or barrel type. Made from cast iron, this stands on little legs, and has a sliding grate in the base for easy ash removal. Air vents speed up the burning process, so the coals are ready to use in 30 minutes. The grill rack can be adjusted to five heights, a bonus in a barbecue that does not have a lid. On occasions when a lid would be useful – to damp down the heat, stop the worst flare-ups from spoiling the food or to smoke fish or chicken – you can improvise by using a large, upturned metal wok, with the wooden handle over the edge so that it does not singe. A domed tent of heavy-duty foil works just as well. Neither needs ventilation holes as the air continues to circulate through the gap between the grill rack and the coals.

The third category of charcoal barbecue is the highly efficient kettle barbecue. It is made from steel with a porcelain enamelled coating, and is usually round with a lid that can be lifted off. There are adjustable air vents in the firebox and the lid, and the ash is usually simple to remove. Spherical kettles come in a range of sizes, from a tiny portable appliance to one that is suitable for cooking a large meal. There are also rectangular kettles, which have hinged lids. They may not have base air vents, but the heat can be adjusted by changing the height of the grill rack.

The main advantage of the kettle barbecue is that direct cooking (immediately over the coals) and indirect cooking (over a drip tray, with the coals raked aside) can both be achieved effortlessly with the lid in place. The lid and the base reflect the heat evenly, so the food develops an all-round golden tan and is cooked evenly, as on a rotisserie. The effect has also been likened to that of oven cooking, and is ideal for large or whole items such as chicken that need long cooking time. There is no need to move the food around, which is important for something that might tear easily, such as stuffed spatchcocked quail. Using the lid for direct cooking ensures that any flare-ups are instantly damped down.

Although the manufacturers advise that the lid should be used, it can be interesting to experiment without it occasionally. Doing so can give food a nice finish. If searing food, do this before closing or adding the lid.

Kettle barbecue handbooks generally suggest that you arrange the coals on either side of the fuel rack, using special holders provided, so that a drip tray can be placed in the centre. It may be better, however, to rake the coals all to one side once the fire is hot, making sure that the space left for the drip tray is level. This not only makes it easier to use direct and indirect cooking methods within the same recipe, but also means that big items such as a whole chicken or a large piece of lamb can be set to one side of the grill rack, freeing the side over the coals for smaller items, such as kebabs or seafood.

gas and electric barbecues Both types are efficient and easy to use, lighting with the touch of a button. Gas ones also give food an authentic barbecue aroma, due to oil and juices dripping on to the ceramic rocks, hot lava rocks, or vitreous enamelled steel bars. If you are considering buying a gas barbecue, try and see it set up first, to ensure that the gas tanks are easy to connect and remove. Also ask about its fuel consumption – some are much more efficient than others.

Electric barbecues are heated by an electric element underneath and usually sit on a table, though larger ones are available. If there isn't a power point near to where you want to cook, you will need an extension cord.

more unusual barbecues Among the many surprising barbecues that exist are tiny terracotta ovens that not only bake and grill, but can also be used in conjunction with a wok. Another favourite is the heavy cast iron barbecue with a fire bed that can be swung into a vertical position. This enables a spit to be positioned in front of the red-hot coals, with a large drip tray set underneath.

Chimineas made of masonry or terracotta are becoming very popular, despite the fact that they have a relatively small area for the fire and grill rack. Solid-style masonry ones have an integral chimney, and are assembled on site. It can be painted the colour you like.

Odd barbecue surprises, like my Arabian punched-tin kebab griller, often turn up in the basements of ethnic stores, or you may find other interesting grills in bric-à-brac shops.

choosing and using a griddle

These are available in various sizes and designs, and are invaluable for indoor grilling. They also transfer happily to the barbecue grill rack, where they are excellent for fragile food or small items that might otherwise slip through the bars. A griddle can also be used to utilize the initial blast of energy from the barbecue, since it provides a buffer between the coals and the food.

The best griddles are made entirely from cast iron though some are cast iron with a hinged metal handle. They can both be used on the stovetop, on the barbecue and in the oven. Some stoves come with sturdy ridged griddles, which sit snugly over a burner in the centre of the hob. The griddle heats along its length, giving you a large cooking area.

It is important that the griddle is searing hot and very dry when the food is first put on it. Test by splashing a few drops of water on the surface; they should evaporate instantly. Oil the food, rather than the pan and, to help reduce the amount of smoke, pat any excess marinade off with kitchen paper. Little oil is needed, which makes the griddle a healthy cooking option. Avoid adding too much oil, or the excess will end up in the grooves and, instead of your food being branded in nice golden tiger stripes, you get oily black lines.

As soon as the food has been seared, lower the heat, or the food will overchar.

grilling equipment

You don't need an extensive store of special equipment for grilling, but a few items will make the task easier and safer.

tools All tools that are going to be used over intense heat should be long-handled and easy to use. Two pairs of tongs are ideal: one for raking and sorting out the coals, and the other for turning and moving the food about. A wide spatula is essential for turning flat items such as steaks. One unconventional but useful piece of barbecue equipment is a pizza server with a long tubular handle. It is perfect for moving large pieces of food such as fish, and banana leaf parcels. Avoid using forks, which will tear fragile foods and cause juices from the food to flow on to the coals.

skewers and spikes A range of skewers in various thicknesses and lengths, as well as cocktail sticks (toothpicks) are vital. Wooden and bamboo skewers need to be pre-soaked in cold water for 30 minutes before use, to prevent them scorching too quickly. Another tip to prevent them burning is to lay the filled skewers on the grill so that exposed ends overlap pieces of meat or vegetable on adjacent skewers. You can easily make your own spikes from thoroughly washed rosemary, apple, cherry or pear twigs and sugarcane spikes also make ideal skewers. Buy sugarcane from ethnic stores or markets, chop through the length carefully using a cleaver or cook's knife, split into 1cm/½in shards and soak for about 1 hour before use.

trays, dishes, grills and racks Have on hand metal trays for conveying food to the barbecue – use separate trays for raw and cooked food. For marinating or salting, you will need shallow, non-corrosive dishes and bowls. (Do not use aluminium or metal ones as they may react to the acid in the marinade.) They should be large enough to hold the food in a single layer. Long, shallow dishes are also handy for soaking wooden skewers.

Hinged wire grills that close completely over the food are useful for small items such as chipolata sausages and burgers, as they can be turned over together. Hinged fish holders are excellent for ensuring that small fish and fillets remain intact when turning. There are also larger ones for fish such as seabass, mackerel or trout, which are cooked whole. Perforated grill baskets are excellent for grilling thinly sliced and small vegetables, such as onions, which might otherwise disappear through the bars of the grill.

Wire or metal racks are extremely useful for improvised beach barbecues. Pick them up in bric-à-brac shops, or use an oven rack.

drip trays and foil When cooking by indirect heat, drip trays are essential for placing under the food to catch the juices. Buy disposable foil trays or use shaped heavy-duty foil. If you can reach the juices in the drip tray easily, use them to baste the food during cooking, or use them afterwards to drizzle over the cooked food when serving. Use your judgement when deciding whether the juices are suitable for this purpose. If meat has cooked for a long time and all that remains is murky fat, then throw it away, but the cooking juices will often have excellent flavour and be well worth using as a sauce.

Make sure you have a good supply of regular and heavy-duty foil. If your barbecue doesn't have a lid, you can make one out of tented heavy-duty foil, or use a wok lid.

brushes A long-handled basting brush is very useful for cooking on a barbecue and a griddle. Herb brushes, made by tying together twigs of thyme, bay, rosemary, savory or sage, are wonderful for basting. Soak them in oil for a few hours beforehand. They will not only flavour the oil used for brushing or basting the ingredients, but the soaked twigs can be burnt afterwards to fill the air with a gentle aroma. When you are barbecueing, a strong wire brush is useful for removing food residue from the grill rack before washing.

other equipment You will also need kitchen paper, string (twine), raffia and long-handled matches.

setting up your barbecue

The best thing about grilling is that anyone can do it, and practice will ensure delicious results every time.

fuel For kindling, use hardwoods such as oak, apple, beech, elm, hornbeam, cherry, pear or plum. Avoid softwoods, especially pine, which gives off a resinous deposit that makes the food bitter. Juniper is different; it adds a nice flavour to food. Woody branches of rosemary, bay and thyme as well as vine cuttings can be used for kindling, and to throw on the barbecue at the end of cooking to flavour the smoke and gently scent the air.

For the primary source of fuel there are several choices. Logs will not last as long as lumpwood charcoal or briquettes, but are perfect for beach barbecues. Lumpwood charcoal, which is wood that has been cooked in a kiln, is ideal for open braziers and portable barbecues. Check the size before you buy, as small pieces can fall through the bars of your barbecue's fuel rack.

Briquettes are made from particles of charcoal mixed with a binder and formed into shapes of a uniform size. They tend to last longer than pieces of lumpwood.

Use briquettes and lumpwood charcoal from sustainably managed forests. These will carry the FSC (Forest Stewardship Council) logo, an independent organisation set up to regulate, amongst other things, the use of trees from forests throughout the world.

firelighters Odourless barbecue firelighter cubes (not the type made for domestic fires) are made without paraffin, and will not taint the food. Two of these, broken in half and pushed into the unlit coals or newspaper under a fire chimney, will be sufficient for the average barbecue. Alternatively, use barbecue lighter gel. This concentrated slime is 100 per cent vegetable in origin, and is quite efficient when squeezed on to the coals and lit with a long match. If you must use lighter fluid, follow the directions carefully and lock it away after use.

getting the heat right An average gas barbecue will be ready to go after about 15 minutes. Charcoal needs longer, and will be ready 30–45 minutes after the fuel has been ignited. There is an art to starting a charcoal barbecue. You will learn to gauge how much fuel to use, but as a guide, a couple of layers of lumpwood charcoal or a packed, single layer of briquettes on the fuel rack will give you sufficient heat to run a barbecue for 1–1½ hours. Heap the fuel up in the centre, using newspaper and twigs underneath as kindling, or one or two firelighters.Do not use more fuel in the belief that the fire will burn for longer: it will be hotter, and will burn just as quickly.

All sorts of wood can be used as fuel for a barbecue, including pieces of bamboo tied with bark, below left, and vine cuttings, centre, which release their aroma into the air as they burn. Drip trays, below right, are essential for preventing small flare-ups caused by meat juices landing on the hot coals.

If you do make an error with quantities and have a large amount of extremely hot coals, dissipate this energy either by using the griddle on the rack, or by protecting foods in a double layer of heavy-duty foil. Spit roasting is the exception – it actually benefits from high temperatures. The meat cooks to a delicious crispness as it turns.

It is not difficult to estimate the heat of the fire by its appearance. When very hot, both lumpwood charcoal and briquettes will glow red, with a light dusting of white or grey ash. At this temperature, thin foods can be seared quickly. These are the right conditions for cooking rare steaks. As the temperature drops to medium, the ash covering gets slightly thicker, with only dots of red showing in places. This is good for most food. When the ash is very thick and powdery, and the coals crumble and collapse when touched, the heat will be low. If extra coals are added at this point, they will ignite and replenish the fire and the coals will take 15–20 minutes to burn down to a useable temperature again. To do this during the cooking, move the grill rack with the food to a tray and cover it while refuelling. Add about half the original amount of coals, return the food and complete the cooking.

changing the temperature The barbecue heat can be altered a little during cooking. To increase the temperature, move the coals to knock off the ash, then pile them up again in the centre of the firebox. If the fire is too hot, carefully spread out the coals and close any air vents in the base for a few minutes. If your barbecue has a lid, use it with the air vents closed to reduce the temperature quickly.

Another way of regulating the heat once the coals have built up a coating of ash is to move the grill rack up and down. This will not work if the coals are red hot, as any unprotected food would quickly turn to carbon, regardless of distance. If you cannot wait for the coals to cool down, rake them aside, put a drip tray in place and cook by indirect heat, with a lid.

If you know you will need to move coals around or to one side at some stage during cooking it is a good idea to start with some coals on each side or on the side you need them on. It's best if you use briquettes rather than lumpwood charcoal as these are easier to move. If the barbecue has air vents in the base, always remember to close them before moving the coals around, and open them again as soon as the coals are positioned.

An easy and safe way to get the fire on a charcoal barbecue going is to use a fire chimney. This is a metal, tube-shaped device that has air holes in the sides. Newspaper is placed in the base, below left, and the space above the paper is filled with coals. When lit with a long-handled match, centre, the newspaper ignites the fuel, which burns swiftly and evenly. When the top coals are dusted with ash, below right, the fire chimney is lifted off, and the hot coals are tipped out to spread evenly across the rack.

well-chosen ingredients

Be aware of the importance of pure, natural and well-sourced food – it will make all the difference to a meal.

It is always worth seeking out the very best ingredients. Whether it is a piece of meat or fish for a main course or the raspberry decoration on a grilled melon dessert, a mediocre item is never going to deliver the same taste sensation as a carefully chosen ingredient that has been produced with care.

Use organic produce whenever possible, buying it from farmers' markets or specialist suppliers of fine, fresh ingredients. If these places aren't nearby, there may be mail order box schemes in your area, which will deliver a range of organic ingredients to your home.

If you are lucky enough to have the time and space, try growing rocket (arugula), fennel, herbs, tomatoes and various edible flowers yourself – even a few pots on the patio can produce wonderful results.

Supermarkets nowadays offer a fabulous selection of ingredients. Always buy fresh ingredients when you can and avoid frozen fish and shellfish that have started thawing as they will have lost all their natural juices and with them their flavour. Also take care when choosing meat – even organic cuts may have been prepared some days earlier.

special items If your store cupboard is well stocked, readying food for an impromptu barbecue will be much easier. Good quality olive oil and chilli oil, vinegars of various types – including champagne, raspberry and rice – and sauces such as tamari and Mexican tomato sauce are good to have on hand, as are spice mixes such as ras el hanout. *Chipotles in adobo* (chillies in sauce) and Japanese wasabi, which is similar to horseradish, will add big bursts of flavour, and dried kombu, arame seaweed and bonito flakes are nutritious as well as adding their distinctive flavour to dishes.

When buying herbs and spices, keep an eye out for unusual items such as Australian aniseed myrtle, Mexican oregano, ground sumac and dried pink rose petals: these add a unique flavour to grilled food.

Banana and pandanus leaves, used for wrapping, are available from Asian markets. Also look out for cooked rice in bamboo and banana leaf parcels. These are a convenient accompaniment, as all you need do is wrap them in foil and heat them over the coals.

breads Middle Eastern flat breads are great for wrapping cooked food and crisping on the grill. Keep items such as round Chinese pancakes, corn and wheat tortilla wraps and ciabatta in the freezer. Even bread sticks are useful for last-minute grilling. For a simple appetizer, serve grilled breadsticks or toast slices of ciabatta on the grill and top with warm chopped tomatoes and olives in oil.

using good ingredients simply There are many quick and easy ways to use good ingredients so they can be served as snacks before a meal or as accompaniments.

Salads can be made with just about any lettuce but look out for mizuna and rocket, which have a great mustardy kick to them.

Add bite to a basic salad dressing with a little tarragon-flavoured mustard, chopped garlic or chilli.

Certain marinades seem to go with just about any dish. Lemon, extra virgin olive oil and garlic is simple but adds great flavour.

Accompany grilled breads, vegetables or chargrilled meats and fish with a few simple savoury butters. Add some chopped herbs and a little garlic or try some finely chopped olives with a splash of lemon juice mixed into softened butter. Pack in small pots and chill until needed.

Put out bowls of cheese cubes, olives, caperberries and sun-dried tomatoes in oil. Baby radishes first dipped in softened butter and then in salt makes the classic French nibble, *radis au beurre*.

Olive oil with chopped herbs and garlic also makes a good dip for bread.

Buy some freshly made hummus, drizzle olive oil over it and dust with paprika. Serve with Lebanese flat bread for a superb snack.

Opposite, clockwise from top left: Just a few of the fabulous ingredients available from around the world, and some easy ideas for using them. Romano peppers, broad beans in the pod, flavoured butters, Kalamata olives, bold bloody Marys, chives with flowers, langoustines, pandanus and banana leaves, and grilled sfilatino bread, centre. Below: Scent finger bowls of water with citrus slices, tea leaves and flower essences such as rose. Float fresh petals on top for a decorative touch.

barbecue techniques

Chefs call it *mise en place* – the work that is done in advance to make the final cooking seem effortless.

Organization is always important in the kitchen, but it is particularly so when outdoor cooking is involved, as everything needs to be ready to cook as soon as the fire reaches the appropriate temperature. All the chopping, marinating, stuffing and skewering can be done in advance to avoid last-minute panics, ensuring that the actual cooking is a relaxing and enjoyable activity.

advance preparation Marinades are very useful for tenderizing and flavouring food, and will keep it moist during cooking. They should enhance the flavour of the food, not overwhelm it, so avoid excessive use of soy sauce, wine or vinegar. When preparing food for the barbecue, avoid marinating beef or chicken in wine as grilling is so rapid that the wine does not have time to cook away.

Yogurt is an excellent tenderizer, as are the juices from kiwi fruit, papaya, citrus fruit such as lemon and lime, and ginger.

Salting is important for flavour when grilling meat, fish or vegetables. This should not be done too soon, or the salt will draw out the moisture, toughening meat and fish. Meat should be salted 30 minutes before cooking; fish and vegetables 15 minutes. Any food that needs to be marinated for a long time should be salted prior to cooking, following the times given above.

If defrosting seafood, do so as close to cooking time as possible. The optimum time for cooking scallops and prawns is when they have just thawed, seconds before the juices start to flow.

grilling The key to successful grilling is to give the food just enough time to allow the heat to penetrate fully to the centre without overcooking the outside. For that barbecued caramelized smokiness, sear the food with a blast of very intense heat for just a short period. Do not leave a large piece of meat over high heat for too long or all the juices will bubble up to the surface, a thick crust will form and blacken and the insides will be cold or, over a longer period, very tough.

Once seared and golden, move the food frequently between cooler and hotter areas of the barbecue for the remainder of the cooking time, or cover with a lid to achieve even cooking. This is essential for meat and vegetables, but also works with fish, giving the skin a lovely golden glow. You can also raise and lower the heat so that the food cooks through without over charring.

before serving Rest meat and fish away from the heat before cutting it up or serving it. Both will continue to cook for a little while anyway, and meat needs the resting time to allow the juices to settle.

The great advantage of grilling is that so much can be done in advance, such as marinating and salting meat and fish, top left and centre. Let meat rest before serving to give the juices time to settle, top right.

safety dos and don'ts

There are a few important rules to bear in mind when playing with fire.

Don't use the starting of a barbecue as a convenient excuse for burning rubbish such as firelighter containers or old charcoal bags. Thick bits of cardboard merely burn down to become thin bits of burnt cardboard, taking to the air and landing on food and in drinks if there is even a hint of a breeze.

Site a barbecue on level ground, well away from overhanging trees and fences. Never leave a lit barbecue unattended, even for a moment, and always keep young children and pets at a safe distance.

Have a bucket of sand handy for major mishaps. Use a water spray sparingly for any small flare-ups, as smoky flames ruin the food with fine sooty particles. To limit flare-ups, lightly oil the grill rack before putting it over the coals and make sure it is very hot before you add the food.

Keep food covered in a cool place until ready to cook. Avoid cross-contamination by keeping raw and cooked food separate.

If using a marinade for basting, make sure the last application is fully cooked before serving. If the marinade is to be used as a sauce, it is safest to make double the amount and use one quantity for marinating and basting, and the other for the sauce.

Use long-handled tools and heatproof mitts to protect your hands when turning food.

Unless food is supposed to be eaten rare, make sure it is completely cooked through. A food thermometer with a probe is good for large or whole pieces of meat. Otherwise you can test with a skewer; when the juices run clear it is done.

Never add lighter fuel to a fire because you think it has gone out – it may merely be dormant, and adding lighter fuel can cause an explosion. Blowing on the coals will usually revive the fire.

At the end of the barbecue, don't snuff out the coals by dousing them with water. This could damage the base of the barbecue irretrievably. Instead, cover with the lid and close any air vents, or spread out the embers and leave them to get cold naturally.

cleaning

Take time to empty and clean out the barbecue firebox after each use, and use a tough wire brush to remove grime from the grill rack. Wash the rack regularly, otherwise your food will acquire black sooty lines rather than the clear golden stripes you are after.

For the same reason, a griddle needs to be cleaned thoroughly after each use. When it has cooled completely, loosen any charred food deposits with a strong wire brush, then wash the griddle with plenty of hot, soapy water. Do not put a griddle that has come straight off the stovetop or barbecue into water or the cast iron might fracture. Dry the griddle well and oil it very lightly before storing until the next use.

Good quality fish, such as this sashimi tuna, top left, needs only a brief searing over a high heat before it is done. Too long and it will overcook. If cooking fish such as salmon, gently flake it with a skewer to see if it is done. If cooking on the beach, top right, take care to douse any discarded embers with water to ensure there are no fire-walking incidents.

almost instant

almost instant

in the time it takes to heat the coals, you can
prepare superb food, ready for the barbecue

Food that is as fast as a 30 minute marinade, or can be tossed together while chilled wine bottles open – that is the guiding rule behind the recipes in this chapter. All the dishes are quick and easy to prepare, and use a limited number of ingredients. Although some preparation could be done in advance, there is no pressure to do so. For example, hot smoked salmon with mango and pineapple mojo may sound elaborate, but is actually very easy to make. By the time you have done the groundwork, the coals will have lost their ferocity and the cooking can begin. Spontaneity is the secret of success for these dishes, many of which make great nibbles or appetizers – the perfect prelude to main dish grills.

toasted sfilatino
with aromatic tomatoes

This is a great way to keep hunger pangs at bay while you wait for the main course. As soon as the barbecue is ready, simply grill the sliced bread, heap on the sauce and drizzle over plenty of good extra virgin olive oil. To accompany, put out little bowls of pine nuts, lightly toasted in a pan over the barbecue.

Serves 6

2 sfilatino (Italian bread sticks), sliced lengthways into 3 pieces

1 garlic clove, cut in half

leaves from 4 fresh oregano sprigs

18 Kalamata olives, slivered off their stones

extra virgin olive oil, for drizzling

ground black pepper

For the aromatic tomatoes

800g/1¾lb ripe plum tomatoes

30ml/2 tbsp extra virgin olive oil

2 garlic cloves, crushed to a paste with a pinch of salt

1 small piece of dried chilli, seeds removed, finely chopped

Prepare the barbecue. Plunge the tomatoes into boiling water for 30 seconds, then refresh in cold water. Peel away the skins, remove the seeds and core and roughly chop the flesh. Mix the oil and crushed garlic in a large frying pan. Place on the stove over a high heat. Once the garlic starts to sizzle, add the tomatoes and the chilli; do not let the garlic burn. Cook for 2 minutes. The aim is to evaporate the liquid rather than pulp the tomatoes, which should keep their shape.

Once the flames have died down, position a lightly oiled grill rack over the hot coals to heat. When the coals are medium-hot, or with a moderate coating of ash, toast the bread on both sides. Generously rub each slice with the cut side of a piece of garlic.

The bread can also be toasted on a hot ridged griddle. Press it down with a spatula to produce the attractive stripes.

Roughly chop all but a few of the oregano leaves and mix them into the tomato sauce. Pile the mixture on to the toasted sfilatino. Scatter over the whole oregano leaves and

the olive slivers. Sprinkle with plenty of pepper, drizzle with lots of olive oil and serve at once.

kefalotyri cubes
spiked with bay leaves

These are delicious with a really cold resinous wine, plenty of excellent olives, fruity olive oil and rustic bread for dipping. They take only minutes to cook and make the perfect pre-dinner snack for a crowd. The lemon and bay leaves are the ideal complement to the hard, salty cheese.

Serves 6

18 large bay leaves or mixed bay and lemon leaves

275g/10oz Kefalotyri or Kasseri cheese, cut into 18 cubes

20ml/4 tsp extra virgin olive oil

ground black pepper

18 short wooden skewers

Soak the wooden skewers in cold water for 30 minutes. Add the bay and/or lemon leaves to the water to prevent them from burning when cooked in the griddle.

Put the cheese cubes in a dish large enough to hold the skewers. Pour over the olive oil. Sprinkle over a little pepper and toss. Drain the skewers, then thread them with the cheese and drained bay leaves and/or lemon leaves. Put the skewers of cheese back in the oil.

Heat a griddle until a few drops of water sprinkled on to the surface evaporate instantly. Lower the heat a little and place the skewers on the griddle, evenly spacing them. Cook for about 5 seconds on each side. The pieces of cheese should have golden-brown lines, and should just be starting to melt. Serve immediately.

Serves 6

30 raw Mediterranean prawns (jumbo shrimp), peeled, with heads removed but tails left on

15ml/1 tbsp sunflower oil

sea salt

30 wooden skewers

For the chilli and raspberry dip

30ml/2 tbsp raspberry vinegar

15ml/1 tbsp sugar

115g/4oz/⅔ cup raspberries

1 large fresh red chilli, seeded and finely chopped

butterfly prawn spiedini
with chilli and raspberry dip

The success of this dish stems from the quality of the prawns, so it is worth getting really good ones, such as Mediterranean prawns, with great flavour and texture. A fruity, slightly spicy dip is such an easy but fabulous accompaniment.

Prepare the barbecue. Soak the skewers in cold water for 30 minutes. Make the dip by mixing the vinegar and sugar in a small pan. Heat gently until the sugar has dissolved, stirring, then add the raspberries.

When the raspberry juices start to flow, tip the mixture into a sieve set over a bowl. Push the raspberries through the sieve using the back of a ladle. Discard the seeds. Stir the chilli into the raspberry purée. When the dip is cool, cover and place in a cool place until needed.

Butterfly each prawn by making an incision down the curved back, just as you would when deveining. Use a piece of kitchen paper to wipe away the dark spinal vein.

These mini kebabs also taste delicious with a vibrant chilli and mango dip. Use one large, ripe mango in place of the raspberries.

Mix the oil with a little sea salt in a bowl. Add the prawns and toss to coat, then thread them on to the drained skewers, spearing them head first. Once the flames have died down, position a lightly oiled grill rack over the coals to heat. When the coals are hot, or with a light coating of ash, grill the prawns for about 5 minutes, depending on size, turning them over once. Serve hot, with the dip.

clams and mussels
in banana leaves

These pretty raffia-tied parcels can either be cooked as soon as they are ready or chilled for up to 30 minutes, offering the cook a moment's respite before the cooking begins. Banana leaves make neat little parcels but they could just as easily be made from double foil.

Heat the oil in a pan and add the chopped onion and garlic with the saffron threads. Cook over a gentle heat for 4 minutes. Add the vermouth and water, increase the heat and simmer for 2 minutes. Stir in the parsley, with salt and pepper to taste. Transfer to a bowl and leave to cool completely.

Tap the clam and mussel shells and discard any that stay open. Stir them into the bowl containing the onion mixture. Trim the hard edge from each banana leaf and discard it. Cut the leaves in half lengthways. Soak them in hot water for 10 minutes, then drain. Wipe any white residue from the leaves. Rinse, then pour over boiling water to soften.

Serves 6

15ml/1 tbsp olive oil

1 large onion, finely chopped

2 garlic cloves, crushed

1.5ml/¼ tsp saffron threads

60ml/4 tbsp Noilly Prat or
other dry vermouth

30ml/2 tbsp water

30ml/2 tbsp chopped fresh
flat leaf parsley

500g/1¼lb clams, scrubbed

900g/2lb cleaned mussels

6 banana leaves

salt and ground black pepper

raffia, for tying

bread sticks, for serving

Top a sheet of foil with a piece of banana leaf, placing it smooth-side up. Place another piece of leaf on top, at right angles, so that the leaves form a cross. Don't worry if the leaves are slightly wet – it's more important to work quickly with the leaves at this stage, while they remain soft and pliable.

Pile one-sixth of the seafood mixture into the centre, then bring up the leaves and tie them into a money-bag shape, using the raffia. Do the same with the foil, scrunching slightly to seal the top. Make the remaining parcels in the same way, then chill the parcels until needed.

Prepare the barbecue. Once the flames have died down, position a lightly oiled grill rack over the coals to heat. When the coals are medium-hot, or with a moderate coating of ash, cook the parcels for about 15 minutes. Carefully remove the outer layer of foil from each and put the parcels back on the grill rack for 1 minute. Transfer to individual plates. The parcels retain heat for a while, so can be left to stand for up to 5 minutes. Untie the raffia and eat from the leaves. Serve with bread sticks, if you wish.

Have a quick peek into one of the bags to make sure the shells have opened before serving. Discard any shellfish that haven't opened.

Serves 4–6

1 fresh fat mild green chilli, seeded and finely chopped

½–1 fresh Scotch bonnet or habanero chilli, seeded and finely chopped

1 small shallot, finely chopped

15ml/1 tbsp clear honey

60ml/4 tbsp olive oil

24 queen scallops on the half shell

salt

2 lemons, cut into thin wedges

chilli and lemon grilled queens

In France during the summertime these little scallops can be found in fish merchants' tanks, balletically propelling themselves about in their pretty pastel pink, yellow and blue shells. Thankfully, they are available elsewhere, too. If you buy queens on the half shell, they are ready to go on to the grill – simplicity itself.

Prepare the barbecue. While it is heating, mix the chillies, shallot, honey and oil in a bowl.

Set out the scallops on a tray. Sprinkle each one with a pinch of salt, then top with a little of the chilli mixture. Once the flames have died down, position a grill rack over the coals to heat. When the coals are medium-hot, or with a moderate coating of ash, place the scallops, on their half shells, on the grill rack.

Cook the scallops for 1½–2 minutes only. If your barbecue has enough space, cook as many as possible at once, moving them from the edge to the centre of the grill rack as necessary. Take care not to overcook them, or they will toughen. Place on a platter, with the lemon wedges for squeezing. Serve immediately.

merguez sausages with iced oysters

This is a truly wonderful taste sensation – revel in the French Christmas tradition of munching on a little hot sausage, then quelling the burning sensation with an ice-cold oyster. Merguez sausages come from North Africa and owe their flavour and colour to harissa, a hot chilli paste with subtle hints of coriander, caraway and garlic.

Serves 6

675g/1½lb merguez sausages

crushed ice for serving

24 oysters

2 lemons, cut into wedges, for squeezing

Prepare the barbecue. Once the flames have died down, position a lightly oiled grill rack over the coals to heat. When the coals are medium-hot, or with a moderate coating of ash, place the sausages on the rack. Grill them for 8 minutes, or until cooked through and golden, turning often.

Meanwhile, spread out the crushed ice on a platter and keep it chilled while you ready the oysters. Make sure all the oysters are tightly closed, and discard any that aren't. Place them on the grill rack, a few at a time, with the deep-side down, so that as they open the juices will be retained in the lower shell. They will begin to ease open after 3–5 minutes and must be removed from the heat immediately, so they don't start to cook.

Lay the oysters on the ice. When they have all eased open, get to work with a sharp knife, opening them fully if need be. Remove the oysters from the flat side of the shell and place them with the juices on the deep half shells. Discard any oysters that fail to open. Serve immediately, with the hot, cooked sausages. Serve with the lemon wedges.

seared mixed onion salad
with parsley and balsamic dressing

This is a fine mix of flavours. On its own, it makes a good vegetarian salad, but it is also delicious served with grilled meat such as beef. Combine as many different onions as you wish; featuring anything from the thuggish fat pink variety sold in West Indian markets to the pink banana shallot, my favourite chopping shallot, which is shaped like a torpedo. Look out also for the elegant reddish purple-and-white spring onions that Italians call *cipolline*.

Serves 4–6

6 red spring onions (scallions), trimmed

6 green salad onions, trimmed and split lengthways

250g/9oz small or baby (pearl) onions, peeled and left whole

2 pink onions, sliced horizontally into 5mm/¼in rounds

2 red onions, sliced into wedges

2 small yellow onions, sliced into wedges

4 banana shallots, halved lengthways

200g/7oz shallots, preferably Thai

45ml/3 tbsp olive oil, plus extra for drizzling

juice of 1 lemon

45ml/3 tbsp chopped fresh flat leaf parsley

30ml/2 tbsp balsamic vinegar

salt and ground black pepper

kuchai flowers (optional), to garnish

Prepare the barbecue. Spread out the onions and shallots in a large flat dish. Whisk the oil and lemon juice together and pour over the mixture. Turn the onions and shallots in the dressing to coat them evenly. Season to taste.

Once the flames have died down, position a grill rack over the coals to heat. When the coals are medium-hot, or covered in a moderate coating of ash, place a griddle or perforated metal vegetable basket on the grill rack to heat, rather than cook directly on the rack and risk losing onions through the gaps in the rack. Grill the onions in batches, for 5–7 minutes, turning them occasionally.

As each batch of onions is cooked, lift them on to a platter and keep hot. Just before serving, add the parsley and gently toss to mix, then drizzle over the balsamic vinegar and extra olive oil.

When available, scatter the whole salad with a few kuchai flowers. These are the lovely blossoms of the evil-smelling Chinese chive. They are available all year round and are sold in Thai food stores.

Garnish with a few kuchai flowers, if you like, and serve with warmed pitta bread and grilled haloumi for a vegetarian starter or with grilled meat or fish as a main course.

grilled fennel salad
with niçoise olives

This is so typically Italian that if you close your eyes you could be on a Tuscan hillside, sitting under a shady tree and enjoying an elegant lunch. Fennel has many fans, but is often used only in its raw state or lightly braised, making this griddle recipe a delightful discovery. For griddle addicts, it is a further proof of that tool's versatility.

Serves 6

3 sweet baby orange (bell) peppers

5 fennel bulbs with green tops, total weight about 900g/2lb

30ml/2 tbsp olive oil

15ml/1 tbsp cider or white wine vinegar

45ml/3 tbsp extra virgin olive oil

24 small niçoise olives

2 long sprigs of fresh savory, leaves removed

salt and ground black pepper

Heat a griddle until a few drops of water sprinkled on to the surface evaporate instantly. Roast the baby peppers, turning them every few minutes until charred all over. Remove the pan from the heat, place the peppers in a bowl and cover with clear film (plastic wrap).

Remove the green fronds from the fennel and reserve. Slice the fennel lengthways into five roughly equal pieces. If the root looks a little tough, cut it out. Place the fennel pieces in a flat dish, coat with the olive oil and season. Rub off the charred skin from the grilled peppers, remove the seeds and cut the flesh into small dice.

Re-heat the griddle and test the temperature again, then lower the heat slightly and grill the fennel slices in batches for about 8–10 minutes, turning frequently, until they are branded with golden grill marks. Monitor the heat so they cook through without over charring. As each batch cooks, transfer it to a flat serving dish.

Whisk the vinegar and olive oil together, then pour the dressing over the fennel. Gently fold in the diced baby orange peppers and the niçoise olives. Tear the savory leaves and fennel fronds and scatter them over the salad. Serve warm or cold.

If cooking directly on the barbecue, char the peppers when the coals are hot, then cool them ready for peeling. Grill the fennel over medium-hot coals and turn frequently once stripes have formed.

4 sweet romano peppers, preferably in mixed colours, total weight about 350g/12oz

90ml/6 tbsp extra virgin olive oil

200g/7oz mozzarella cheese

10 drained bottled sweet cherry peppers, finely chopped

115g/4oz ricotta salata

30ml/2 tbsp chopped fresh oregano leaves

24 black olives

2 garlic cloves, crushed

salt and ground black pepper

dressed mixed salad leaves and bread, to serve

sweet romanos stuffed
with two cheeses and cherry peppers

Romanos are wonderful Mediterranean peppers. They are long, pointy and slightly gnarled, and look a little like a large poblano chilli. Not hot but delightfully sweet, they also go by the names Romiro or extra sweet. Their flavour is nicely balanced by the ricotta salata, a mature dried and slightly salty version of the popular cheese.

Prepare the barbecue. Split the peppers lengthways and remove the seeds and membrane. Rub 15ml/1 tbsp of the oil all over the peppers. Place them hollow-side uppermost.

Slice the mozzarella and divide equally among the pepper halves. Scatter over the chopped cherry peppers, season lightly and crumble the ricotta salata over the top, followed by the oregano leaves and olives. Mix the garlic with the remaining oil and add a little salt and pepper. Spoon about half the mixture over the filling in the peppers.

Once the flames have died down, rake the coals to one side. Position a lightly oiled grill rack over the coals to heat. When the coals are medium-hot, or with a moderate coating of ash, place the filled peppers on the section of grill rack that is not over the coals. Cover with a lid, or improvise with a wok lid or tented heavy-duty foil. Grill for 6 minutes, then spoon the remaining oil mixture over the filling, replace the lid and continue to grill for 6–8 minutes more, or until the peppers are lightly charred and the cheese has melted. Serve with a dressed green or leafy salad and bread.

grilled potatoes
with chive flower dressing

There is something very enjoyable about using edible flowering plants and herbs from the garden. Grabbing a handful of this herb or that flower is all part of the creativity of cooking and eating outdoors, and can produce really exciting and unexpected results.

Serves 4–6

900g/2lb salad potatoes, such as charlottes, Jersey royals or French ratte

15ml/1 tbsp champagne vinegar

105ml/7 tbsp olive oil

45ml/3 tbsp chopped chives

about 10 chive flowers

4–6 small bunches yellow cherry tomatoes on the vine

salt and ground black pepper

Prepare the barbecue. Boil the potatoes in a large pan of lightly salted water for about 10 minutes, or until just tender. Meanwhile make the dressing by whisking the vinegar with 75ml/5 tbsp of the oil, then stirring in the chives and flowers. Drain the potatoes and cut them in half horizontally. Season to taste.

Once the flames have died down, position a grill rack over the coals to heat. When the coals are medium-hot, or with a moderate coating of ash, toss the potatoes in the remaining oil and lay them on the grill rack, cut-side down. Leave for about 5 minutes, then press down a little so that they are imprinted with the marks of the grill.

Turn the potatoes over and cook the second side for about 3 minutes. Place the potatoes in a bowl, pour over the dressing and toss lightly to mix.

Grill the tomatoes for 3 minutes, or until they are just beginning to blister. Serve with the potatoes, which can be hot, warm or cold.

yellow courgette wraps
with spinach and mozzarella

This is a good first course or accompaniment, especially useful for gardeners with a glut of courgettes. You need the large ones that have been growing sneakily under the leaves. They should measure about 19cm/7½in. A barbecue with an adjustable grill is ideal for this recipe, as the wraps need to be seared quickly at the end.

Serves 6

2 large yellow courgettes (zucchini), total weight about 675g/1½lb

45ml/3 tbsp olive oil

250g/9oz baby leaf spinach

250g/9oz mini mozzarella balls

salad burnet, rocket (arugula) and mizuna leaves, to garnish (optional)

For the dressing

2 whole, unpeeled garlic cloves

30ml/2 tbsp white wine vinegar

30ml/2 tbsp olive oil

15ml/1 tbsp extra virgin olive oil

45ml/3 tbsp walnut oil

salt and ground black pepper

Prepare the barbecue. To make the dressing, place the garlic in a small pan with water to cover. Bring to the boil, lower the heat and simmer for 5 minutes. Drain. When cool enough to handle, pop the garlic cloves out of their skins and crush to a smooth paste with a little salt. Scrape into a bowl and add the vinegar. Whisk in the oils and season to taste.

Slice each courgette lengthways into six or more broad strips, about 3mm/⅛in wide. Lay them on a tray. Set aside 5ml/1 tsp of the oil and brush the rest over the courgette strips, evenly coating them with the oil.

Place a wok over a high heat. When it starts to smoke, add the reserved oil and stir-fry the spinach for 30 seconds, or until just wilted. Tip into a sieve and drain well, then pat dry the leaves with kitchen paper. Tear or slice the mozzarella balls in half and place on kitchen paper to drain.

Once the flames have died down, position a lightly oiled grill rack over the coals to heat. When the coals are medium-hot, or with a moderate coating of ash, lay the courgettes on the rack. Grill on one side only for 2–3 minutes, or until striped golden. As each strip cooks, return it to the tray, grilled-side up.

Place small heaps of spinach towards one end of each courgette strip. Lay two pieces of mozzarella on each pile of spinach. Season well.

Using a metal spatula, carefully transfer the topped strips, a few at a time, back to the barbecue rack and grill for about 2 minutes, or until the underside of each is striped with golden-brown grill marks.

The three leaves suggested make a really tasty garnish. Salad burnet has a slightly nutty flavour, with subtle hints of cucumber, and combines perfectly with peppery rocket and mild, mustardy mizuna.

When the cheese starts to melt, fold the plain section of each courgette over the filling to make a wrap. Lift off carefully and drain on kitchen paper. Serve with the garnish of salad leaves, if you like, and drizzle the dressing over the top.

roasted vegetable quesadillas
with melted mozzarella

This recipe is a wonderful example of how the griddle and grill rack can be used simultaneously to cope with a range of ingredients. Have a long griddle on one side of the grill rack for the onions and peppers; the aubergines can cook over the coals on the other side.

Prepare a barbecue. Once the flames have died down, position a lightly oiled grill rack over the hot coals to heat. When the coals are hot to medium-hot, or with a light to moderate coating of ash, heat a griddle until a few drops of water sprinkled on the surface evaporate instantly.

Toss the peppers, onions and aubergines in the oil on a large baking tray. Place the peppers, skin-side down, on the griddle or directly on the grill rack and cook until seared and browned underneath. If the food starts to char, remove the griddle until the coals cool down. Put the peppers in a bowl, cover with clear film (plastic wrap) and set aside.

Grill the onions and aubergines until they have softened slightly and are branded with brown grill marks, then set them aside. Rub the skins off the peppers with your fingers, cut each piece in half and add to the other vegetables.

Cut the mozzarella into 20 slices. Place them, along with the roasted vegetables, into a large bowl and add the chillies and tomato sauce. Stir well to mix, and season with salt and pepper to taste. Place the griddle over a medium heat and cook all the tortillas on one side only.

The quesadillas can be cut into wedges and eaten as they come off the griddle or wrapped in foil to keep warm while the rest are cooked.

Lay a tortilla on the griddle, cooked-side up, and pile about a quarter of the vegetable mixture into the centre of the tortilla. Scatter over some basil leaves. When the tortilla browns underneath, put another tortilla on top, cooked-side down. Carefully turn the quesadilla over using a wide pizza server with tubular handle and continue to cook until the underside has browned and the cheese just starts to melt. Remove from the pan with the pizza server and serve immediately, or wrap in foil to keep warm while you cook the remaining quesadillas.

Serves 6–8

1 yellow and 1 orange (bell) pepper, each quartered and seeded

2 red (bell) peppers, quartered and seeded

2 red onions, cut into wedges with root intact

8 long baby aubergines (eggplant), total weight about 175g/6oz, halved lengthways

30ml/2 tbsp olive oil

400g/14oz block mozzarella cheese

2 fresh green chillies, seeded and sliced into rounds

15ml/1 tbsp Mexican tomato sauce

8 corn or wheat flour tortillas

handful of fresh basil leaves

salt and ground black pepper

lamb and ras el hanout kebabs
with mint chutney

These little round lamb kebabs owe their exotic flavour to ras el hanout, a North African spice, which has to be the sexiest the world has to offer. Its hedonistic qualities are achieved by adding highly perfumed dried damask rose petals to over ten different spices to make a mix that each vendor claims for his own. The dried pink rose petals can be found in Moroccan and Middle Eastern stores.

Serves 4–6

30ml/2 tbsp extra virgin olive oil

1 onion, finely chopped

2 garlic cloves, crushed

35g/1¼oz/5 tbsp pine nuts

500g/1¼lb/2½ cups minced (ground) lamb

10ml/2 tsp ras el hanout spice mix

10ml/2 tsp dried pink rose petals (optional)

salt and ground black pepper

18 short wooden or metal skewers

For the fresh mint chutney

40g/1½oz/1½ cups fresh mint leaves

10ml/2 tsp sugar

juice of 2 lemons

2 eating apples, peeled and finely grated

To serve (optional)

150ml/¼ pint/⅔ cup Greek (US strained plain) yogurt

7.5ml/1½ tsp rose harissa

If using wooden skewers, soak 18 skewers in cold water for 30 minutes. Heat the oil in a frying pan on the stove. Add the onion and garlic and fry gently for 7 minutes. Stir in the pine nuts. Fry for about 5 minutes more, or until the mixture is slightly golden, then set aside to cool.

Make the fresh mint chutney. Chop the mint finely by hand or in a food processor, then add the sugar, lemon juice and grated apple. Stir or pulse to mix.

Prepare the barbecue. Place the minced lamb in a large bowl and add the ras el hanout and rose petals, if using. Tip in the cooled onion mixture and add salt and pepper. Using your hands, mix well, then form into 18 balls. Drain the skewers and mould a ball on to each one.

Once the flames have died down, rake a few hot coals to one side. Position a lightly oiled grill rack over the coals to heat.

When the coals are cool, or with a thick coating of ash, place the kebabs on the grill over the part with the most coals. If it is easier, cover the barbecue with a lid or tented heavy-duty foil so that the heat will circulate and they will cook evenly all over. Otherwise, you will need to stay with them, turning them frequently for about 10 minutes. This prevents the kebabs from forming a hard crust before the meat is cooked right through to the centre. Serve with the yogurt, mixed with the rose harissa, if you like. They can also be wrapped in Middle Eastern flat bread such as lavash with a green salad and cucumber slices piled in with them.

You can also cook these kebabs on a hot griddle. They will take about 10 minutes. Sear on a high heat then lower the heat and turn frequently.

steak ciabatta
with hummus and salad

The all-time favourite with my family, this tastes all the better when enjoyed on a beach after an afternoon spent battling the surf. Portable barbecues become a way of life with children around. At the end of a hectic day, when tiredness and chills are just setting in, there is only one thing that beats the fun of lighting a fire, and that is devouring the delectable food you have cooked on it.

Serves 4

2 romaine lettuce hearts

3 garlic cloves, crushed to a paste with enough salt to season the steaks

30ml/2 tbsp extra virgin olive oil

4 sirloin steaks, 2.5cm/1in thick, total weight about 900g/2lb

4 small ciabatta breads

salt and ground black pepper

For the dressing

10ml/2 tsp Dijon mustard

5ml/1 tsp cider or white wine vinegar

15ml/1 tbsp olive oil

For the hummus

400g/14oz can chickpeas, drained and rinsed

45ml/3 tbsp tahini

2 garlic cloves, crushed

juice of 1 lemon

30ml/2 tbsp water

60ml/4 tbsp extra virgin olive oil

To make the hummus, place the chickpeas in a food processor and pulse briefly to form a paste. Add the tahini, garlic and lemon juice, with salt and pepper to taste. Pour in the water and pulse to mix. Scrape into a container or jar and pour the extra virgin olive oil over the surface. Cover, then put in a cool place until ready to use.

Separate the romaine leaves and clean them. Put into an airtight container until ready to use. Make a dressing for the salad by mixing the mustard and vinegar in a small jar. Gradually whisk in the oil, then season to taste.

Mix the crushed garlic and oil together in a shallow dish. Add the steaks and rub the mixture into both surfaces. Cover and leave in a cool place until ready to cook.

This recipe can be easily prepared in the morning before heading off on a picnic. The hummus and dressing need only to be kept in jars in a cool place, and the romaine lettuce can be prepared, too.

Prepare the barbecue. Once the flames have died down, position a lightly oiled grill rack over the coals to heat. When the coals are hot, or with a light coating of ash, transfer the steaks to the grill rack. For rare meat, cook the steaks for 2 minutes on one side, without moving, then turn over and grill the other side for 3 minutes. For medium steaks, cook for 4 minutes on each side. Transfer to a plate, cover loosely and leave to rest for 2 minutes.

Dress the romaine leaves. Split each ciabatta. Place the ciabatta cut-side down on the grill rack for a minute to heat. Spread the hummus, with any oil, on the bottom half of each ciabatta. Slice the steaks and arrange on top of the hummus, with some of the leaves. Replace the lids and cut each filled ciabatta in half to serve.

stuffed corn-fed chicken breast
marinated in maple and lemon

This is one of those dishes that makes you feel good about cooking for friends. It does not require any effort but looks and tastes as if you have gone to huge amounts of trouble. Serve grilled Mediterranean vegetables, or use simply dressed salad leaves with the chicken.

Serves 4–6

4–6 boneless chicken breast portions, preferably from a corn-fed bird

115g/4oz firm goat's cheese

60ml/4 tbsp chopped fresh oregano

20ml/4 tsp maple syrup

juice of 1 lemon

oil for brushing

salt and ground black pepper

Slash a pocket horizontally in each chicken portion. Mix the goat's cheese, chopped oregano and 10ml/2 tsp of the maple syrup in a small bowl. Stuff the pockets in the chicken with the mixture. Don't overfill.

Put the remaining maple syrup into a shallow dish large enough to hold the chicken portions in a single layer. Stir in the lemon juice and add the chicken portions. Rub them all over with the mixture, then cover and leave in a cool place for 20 minutes, turning them occasionally. Season with salt and pepper and marinate for 10 minutes more.

Prepare the barbecue. Once the flames have died down, rake the hot coals to one side and insert a drip tray flat beside them. Position a lightly oiled grill rack over the coals to heat. When the coals are hot, or with a light coating of ash, lay the chicken breast portions, skin-side up, on the grill rack over the drip tray. Cover with a lid or tented heavy-duty foil.

You can cook these successfully on a hot griddle. They will take about 20 minutes. Sear on a high heat then lower the heat. Turn frequently.

Grill the chicken for about 15 minutes in total, turning and moving the pieces around the grill rack so that they cook evenly without getting too charred. Baste with any remaining marinade 5 minutes before the end of cooking.

Transfer the chicken to a dish to rest and keep warm for about 5 minutes before serving.

rare gingered duck
with sweet tare

This recipe came about by accident, like so many that are the result of putting together whatever is in the cupboard or the freezer. It is essentially Japanese, thanks to the tare, or sauce, but why not cross cultures and serve the duck with Chinese pancakes, spring onions and cucumber. If you want to be a purist serve the duck with soba (buckwheat noodles) instead of the pancakes.

Make four slashes in the skin of each duck breast fillet, then lay them skin-side up on a plate. Squeeze the grated ginger over the duck to extract every drop of juice; discard the pulp. Generously rub the juice all over the duck, especially into the slashes. Using a vegetable peeler, peel the cucumber in strips, then cut it in half, scoop out the seeds and chop the flesh. Set aside in a bowl.

To make the tare, mix the tamari, mirin and sugar in a heavy pan and heat gently together until the sugar has dissolved. Increase the heat and simmer for 4–5 minutes, or until the sauce has reduced by about one-third and become syrupy.

Heat a griddle on the stove over a high heat until a few drops of water sprinkled on to the surface evaporate instantly. Sear the duck breasts, in batches if necessary, placing them skin-side down.

Serves 4

4 large duck breast fillets, total weight about 675g/1½lb

5cm/2in piece of fresh root ginger, finely grated

½ large cucumber

12 Chinese pancakes

6 spring onions (scallions), finely shredded

For the tare

105ml/7 tbsp tamari

105ml/7 tbsp mirin

25g/1oz/2 tbsp sugar

salt and ground black pepper

When the fat has been rendered, and the skin is nicely browned, remove the duck from the pan. Drain off the fat and wipe the pan clean with kitchen paper. Reheat it, return the duck, flesh-side down and cook over a medium heat for about 3 minutes.

Brush on a little of the tare, turn the duck over, brush the other side with tare and turn again. This should take about 1 minute, by which time the duck should be cooked rare; when pressed, there should be some give in the flesh. Remove from the pan and let the duck rest for a few minutes before slicing each breast across at an angle.

Warm the pancakes in a steamer for about 3 minutes. Serve with the duck, *tare*, spring onions and cucumber.

To cook on the barbecue, position the duck on the grill rack over a large drip tray. Cook over hot coals, covered with a lid or tented heavy-duty foil. Follow the timings given left.

hot smoked salmon
with mango and pineapple mojo

This is a fantastic way of smoking fish on a charcoal barbecue, using soaked hickory wood chips. Mojo, a spicy but not hot sauce popular in Cuba, is perfect to cut the richness of the hot smoked salmon.

Serves 6

6 salmon fillets, about 175g/6oz each, with skin

15ml/1 tbsp sunflower oil

salt and ground black pepper

2 handfuls hickory wood chips, soaked in cold water for at least 30 minutes

For the mojo

1 ripe mango, diced

4 drained canned pineapple slices, diced

1 small red onion, fincly chopped

1 fresh long mild red chilli, seeded and finely chopped

15ml/1 tbsp good quality sweet chilli sauce

grated rind and juice of 1 lime

leaves from 1 small lemon basil plant or 45ml/3 tbsp fresh coriander (cilantro) leaves, chopped

Place the salmon fillets, skin-side down, on a platter. Sprinkle the flesh lightly with salt. Cover and leave in a cool place for about 30 minutes.

Make the mojo by putting the mango, pineapple slices, onion and chilli in a bowl. Add the chilli sauce, lime rind and juice, and the herb leaves. Stir to mix well. Cover tightly and leave in a cool place until needed.

Prepare the barbecue. Pat the salmon fillets with kitchen paper, then brush each one with a little oil. Once the flames have died down, position a lightly oiled grill rack over the coals to heat. When the coals are medium-hot, and with a moderate coating of ash, add the salmon fillets, placing them on the rack skin-side down. Cover the barbecue with a lid or tented heavy-duty foil and cook the fish for about 3 minutes.

Drain the hickory chips into a colander and sprinkle about a third of them as evenly as possible over the coals. Carefully drop them through the grill racks, taking care not to scatter the ash as you do so.

When sweet pineapples are in season, use them fresh in the mojo. You will need about half a medium-sized pineapple. Slice off the skin, remove the core and cut into chunks.

Replace the barbecue cover and continue cooking for a further 8 minutes, adding a small handful of hickory chips twice more during this time. Serve the salmon hot or cold, with the mojo.

strawberries and marshmallows
on cherry wood spikes

It is always a treat to have permission to eat marshmallows. After cooking, dredge these little kebabs with loads of icing sugar, some of which will melt into the strawberry juice. The grill has to be very hot to sear the marshmallows quickly before they have a chance to melt.

Serves 4

16 mixed pink and white marshmallows, chilled

16 strawberries

icing (confectioners') sugar for dusting

8 short lengths of cherry wood or metal skewers

Prepare the barbecue. If you are using cherry wood skewers, soak them in water for 30 minutes. When the coals are hot or with a light coating of ash, lightly oil the grill rack and position it just above the coals to heat. Spike two marshmallows and two strawberries on each drained cherry wood or metal skewer and grill over the hot coals for 20 seconds on each side. If nice grill marks don't appear easily, don't persist for too long – cook until the marshmallows are warm and just beginning to melt.

Transfer the skewered strawberries and marshmallows to individual dessert plates or a large platter, dust generously with icing sugar and serve.

honey-seared melon
with lavender and raspberries

This fabulously simple dessert came about one summer evening, with the lavender in flower and a bowl of strongly scented raspberries to hand. The melon was slightly underripe and needed sweetening. Honeycomb did the trick, and it's hard to imagine this dish without it now.

Serves 6

1.3kg/3lb melon, preferably Charentais

200g/7oz honeycomb

5ml/1 tsp water

a bunch of lavender, plus extra flowers for decoration

300g/11oz/2 cups raspberries

Cut the melon in half, scoop out the seeds then cut each half into 3 slices. Put a third of the honey in a bowl and dilute it by stirring in the water. Make a brush with the lavender and dip it in the honey.

Heat a griddle until a few drops of water sprinkled on to the surface evaporate instantly. Lightly brush the melon with the honey mixture. Grill for 30 seconds on each side. Serve with the raspberries, honeycomb and lavender flowers.

a little ahead

a little ahead

these recipes delight in fresh ingredients and glorious ease of preparation and presentation

The prime attraction of the following recipes is that they can be prepared in stages to help the cook get well ahead before the actual cooking begins. A little chopping, a few moments making a marinade – such things ease the path of the person producing the meal. These recipes involve a few more ingredients and have slightly more complex flavours than those in the first section. Dishes are intended to be eaten on the day they are made, but can wait a while between preparation and grilling. The rempah rempah burgers, for example, are chilled briefly to set the creamed coconut that gives them their inimitable flavour and, when preparing patra ni macchi, you can make the banana leaf parcels at your leisure, then chill them until you are ready to pop them on the barbecue when the guests arrive.

walnut bread with hunkar begendi and marinated olives

This Turkish dish consists of grilled mashed aubergine with cheese. The flour and milk have been omitted from this version, which may be sacrilege, but it does give a lighter result. If you want to buy the marinated olives that's fine, but it is an enjoyable process to do it yourself, steeping the olives with various flavourings in a good quality oil. The oil can then be used to make the hunkar begendi.

Serves 8

3 aubergines (eggplant), total weight about 675g/1½lb, cut widthways into 5mm/¼in slices

60ml/4 tbsp finely grated Kefalotyri or Kasseri cheese

juice of ½ lemon

1 loaf walnut bread, sliced as thinly as possible

extra virgin olive oil, for brushing

salt and ground black pepper

For the marinated olives

175g/6oz/1 cup olives of various colours

fennel seeds or dried fennel seed heads and ground black pepper

fresh hot chillies and rosemary sprigs

lemon slices and fresh thyme branches

120ml/4fl oz/½ cup extra virgin olive oil

To make the marinated olives, divide them among three bowls and add a different flavouring combination to each: try the fennel seeds and pepper with mixed olives, the chillies and rosemary with black olives, and the lemon and thyme with green olives. Divide the oil among the bowls and leave to stand for at least several hours. Heat a griddle until a few drops of water sprinkled on to the surface evaporate instantly.

Brush the aubergine slices with some of the oil from the olives and grill for 5 minutes, or until soft and branded with grill marks on both sides. Tip into a small bowl and mash to a rough pulp. While the mixture is still hot, add the finely grated cheese and lemon juice and stir well to mix through, with salt and pepper to taste. Drain most of the oil from the olives and mix it into the pulp. Cover the hunkar begendi and put in a cool place until needed.

Brush the bread slices sparingly with oil on one side and toast on the griddle or on an oiled grill rack over a barbecue, if it is prepared already for another dish. Keep an eye on the toast because it just needs to become crisp not blacken.

Serve the toast with small bowls of hunkar begendi and the marinated olives.

This dish is great served as an appetizer before a slow-cooking main course. Get the food for that one going, then cook the aubergines beside it on the grill rack.

corn tostaditas
with salsa and guacamole

This is just the right snack to keep hungry guests from feeling the effects of too much preprandial alcohol. It is best if you make the tostaditas using a griddle either on the barbecue or on the stovetop. Not only do you get those wonderfully defined black tiger stripes but you also have more control than when cooking directly on a grill rack over a hot barbecue.

Serves 6

30ml/2 tbsp chipotle or other chilli oil

15ml/1 tbsp sunflower oil

8 yellow corn tortillas, total weight about 300g/11oz

For the salsa

4 tomatoes

30ml/2 tbsp chopped fresh basil

juice of ½ lime

20ml/4 tsp good quality sweet chilli sauce

1 small red onion, finely chopped (optional)

salt and ground black pepper

For the guacamole

4 avocados

juice of ½ lime

1 fresh fat mild chilli, seeded and finely chopped

Make the salsa one or two hours ahead if possible, to allow the flavours to blend. Cut the tomatoes in half, remove the cores and scoop out most of the seeds. Dice the flesh. Add the chopped basil, lime juice and sweet chilli sauce. Stir in the onion, if using, then add salt and pepper to taste.

Make the guacamole. Cut the avocados in half, prize out the stones, then scoop the flesh into a bowl. Add the lime juice, chopped chilli and seasoning. Mash with a fork to a fairly rough texture.

Prepare the barbecue. Mix the chilli and sunflower oils together. Stack the tortillas on a board. Lift the first tortilla off the stack and brush it lightly with the oil mixture. Turn it over and place it on the board, then brush the exposed side with oil. Repeat with the remaining tortillas, to make a new, second stack. When finished, slice the whole stack diagonally into six fat pointed triangles.

Reserve one of the avocado stones to bury in the guacamole mixture. This, along with the lime juice, will help to stop the mixture from discolouring.

Once the flames have died down, position a lightly oiled grill rack over the hot coals to heat. When the coals are hot, or with a light coating of ash, heat a griddle on the grill rack until a few drops of water sprinkled on to the surface evaporate instantly. Grill a few tostaditas at a time for 30 seconds each side, pressing down for good contact with the griddle.

Transfer them to a bowl, so that they are supported by its sides. As they cool, they will shape themselves to the curve of the bowl. Serve with the salsa and guacamole.

Serves 4–8

8 sardines, total weight about 800g/1¾lb, scaled and gutted

50g/2oz/¼ cup salt

focaccia, to serve

oil, for brushing

For the salmoriglio

5ml/1 tsp sea salt flakes

60ml/4 tbsp chopped fresh tarragon leaves

40g/1½oz/generous 1 cup chopped flat leaf parsley

1 small red onion, very finely chopped

105ml/7 tbsp extra virgin olive oil

60ml/4 tbsp lemon juice

salted and grilled sardines

Whole grilled sardines are classic Mediterranean beach food, evoking memories of lazy lunches under rustic awnings, just a step away from the sea. Here they are served with salmoriglio, an Italian herb salsa pounded with sea salt. They can also be cooked on skewers over a dying fire.

Rub the sardines inside and out with salt. Cover and put in a cool place for 30–45 minutes. Make the salmoriglio by adding the salt to a mortar and pounding all the ingredients one at a time with a pestle.

Meanwhile, prepare the barbecue. Rinse the salt off the sardines. Pat them dry with kitchen paper, then leave to air-dry for 15 minutes. Once the flames have died down, position a lightly oiled grill rack over the coals to heat.

When the coals are cool, or with a thick coating of ash, brush the fish with a little oil and put them in a small, hinged, wire barbecue fish basket. If you don't have a wire basket, grill directly on the rack, but oil it well first. Grill for about 3 minutes on one side and about 2½ minutes on the other. Serve with the salmoriglio and focaccia.

aubergine and butternut salad
with crumbled feta

This delightful salad is all the reason you need to get the griddle out in the colder months. Not only do the colour combinations please the eye, but the flavours really work. Look out for slivered pistachios in Middle Eastern shops: they combine brilliantly with the orange butternut.

Serves 4

2 aubergines (eggplant)

1 butternut squash, about 1kg/2¼lb, peeled

120ml/4fl oz/½ cup extra virgin olive oil

5ml/1 tsp paprika

150g/5oz feta cheese

50g/2oz/⅓ cup pistachio nuts, roughly chopped

salt and ground black pepper

Slice the aubergines widthways into 5mm/¼in rounds. Spread them out on a tray and sprinkle with a little salt. Leave for 30 minutes. Slice the squash in the same way, scooping out any seeds with a spoon. Place the butternut squash slices in a bowl, season lightly and toss with 30ml/2 tbsp of the oil.

Heat the griddle until a few drops of water sprinkled on to the surface evaporate instantly. Lower the heat a little and grill the butternut squash slices in batches. Sear for about 1½ minutes on each side, then put them on a tray. Continue until all the slices have been cooked, then dust with a little of the paprika.

Pat the aubergine slices dry. Toss with the remaining oil and season lightly. Cook in the same way as the squash. When all the slices are cooked, mix the aubergine and squash together in a bowl. Crumble the feta over the warm salad, scatter the chopped pistachio nuts over the top and dust with the remaining paprika.

grilled halloumi and bean salad
with skewered potatoes

Halloumi is that hard, white, salty goat's milk cheese that squeaks when you bite it. It grills really well and is the perfect complement to the lovely fresh-tasting flavours of the vegetables. This salad can be grilled on the stovetop, but if you are planning to use the barbecue for another dish, use that, and take advantage of the initial hot blast of heat from the coals.

Serves 4

20 baby new potatoes, total weight about 300g/11oz

200g/7oz extra fine green beans, trimmed

675g/1½lb broad (fava) beans, shelled (shelled weight about 225g/8oz)

200g/7oz halloumi cheese, cut into 5mm/¼in slices

1 garlic clove, crushed to a paste with a large pinch of salt

90ml/6 tbsp olive oil

5ml/1 tsp cider vinegar or white wine vinegar

15g/½oz/½ cup fresh basil leaves, shredded

45ml/3 tbsp chopped fresh savory

2 spring onions (scallions), finely sliced

salt and ground black pepper

4 metal or wooden skewers

Thread five potatoes on to each skewer, and cook in a large pan of salted boiling water for about 7 minutes, or until almost tender. Add the green beans and cook for 3 minutes more. Tip in the broad beans and cook for just 2 minutes. Drain all the vegetables in a large colander. Remove the potatoes, still on their skewers, from the colander, then refresh the cooked broad beans under plenty of cold running water. Pop each broad bean out of its skin to reveal the bright green inner bean. Place the beans in a bowl, cover and set aside.

Place the halloumi slices and the potato skewers in a wide dish. Whisk the garlic and oil together with a generous grinding of black pepper. Add to the dish and toss the halloumi and potato skewers in the mixture. Once the flames have died down, rake the coals over to one side. Position a grill rack over the coals to heat.

This dish can be cooked directly on the barbecue. When the coals are medium-hot, sear the vegetables and cheese for 2 minutes on each side.

When the coals are hot, or with a light coating of ash, heat a griddle until a few drops of water sprinkled on to the surface evaporate instantly. Place the cheese and potato skewers in the griddle and cook over the coals for about 2 minutes on each side. If they over-char, move the griddle to the cooler side of the grill rack.

Add the vinegar to the oil and garlic remaining in the dish and whisk to mix. Toss in the beans, herbs and spring onions, with the cooked halloumi. Serve, with the potato skewers laid alongside.

grilled vegetables
with bagna cauda

Bagna cauda means "warm bath" and this rich dip is the traditional Piedmontese accompaniment to raw or cooked vegetables. It is usually kept warm in an earthenware dish over a candle heater, but the edge of a waning barbecue is also ideal. In this recipe, it is teamed with an assortment of grilled root vegetables though other vegetables also work well. Along with some good-looking crusty Italian bread, put out plenty of young red wine – such delicious food makes for thirsty work.

Serves 4–6

4 small sweet potatoes, total weight about 675g/1½lb

4 carrots, total weight about 375g/13oz

parsnips, total weight about 400g/14oz

4 raw beetroot (beets), total weight about 400g/14oz

450g/1lb asparagus, trimmed

60ml/4 tbsp extra virgin olive oil

salt and ground black pepper

For the bagna cauda

3–4 garlic cloves, crushed

50–65g/2–2½oz drained anchovy fillets, chopped

25g/1oz/2 tbsp unsalted (sweet) butter, melted

200ml/7fl oz/scant 1 cup extra virgin olive oil

Prepare the barbecue. Cutting lengthways, slice each sweet potato and carrot into 8 pieces, each parsnip into 7 and each beetroot into 10. Toss all the vegetables except the beetroot in most of the oil on a big tray. Put the beetroot on a separate tray as it might otherwise bleed over all the other vegetables. Gently toss the beetroot in the remaining oil and season all the vegetables well.

This dish can be cooked on a griddle either inside on the stovetop or positioned over the barbecue. Follow the timings given below for either method.

Make the bagna cauda. Place the garlic, anchovies and butter, with a little pepper, into a food processor. Pour in 30ml/2 tbsp of the oil and whizz to a purée. With the motor running, add the remaining oil. Tip into a heatproof bowl or pan and warm very gently at the edge of the barbecue or over a pan of simmering water when ready to serve.

Once the flames have died down, position a lightly oiled grill rack over the coals to heat. When the coals are medium-hot, or with a moderate coating of ash, arrange the vegetables over the grill rack.

Lightly grill the vegetables for 3 minutes on each side, or until tender and branded with dark golden grill lines. Remove them as they cook and serve hot or warm with the warm bagna cauda.

Serves 6–8

2 pork tenderloins, each about 350g/12oz

45ml/3 tbsp olive oil

40g/1½oz/1½ cups fresh basil leaves, chopped

50g/2oz Pecorino cheese, grated

2.5ml/½ tsp chilli flakes

salt and ground black pepper

basil and pecorino stuffed pork tenderloin

This is a very easy dish to make and looks extremely impressive. It is good for a bulk cookout as you can get several tenderloins on a barbecue grill, and each one yields about eight chunky slices. Serve with a chickpea salad topped with finely chopped onions and parsley, and flavoured with a really mustardy dressing.

Make a 1cm/½in slit down the length of one of the tenderloins. Continue to slice, cutting along the fold of the meat, until you can open it out flat. Lay between two sheets of baking parchment and pound with a rolling pin to an even thickness of about 1cm/½in. Lift off the top sheet of parchment and brush the meat with a little oil. Press half the basil leaves on to the surface, then scatter over half the Pecorino cheese and chilli flakes. Add a little pepper.

Roll up lengthways to form a sausage and tie with kitchen string (twine). Repeat with the second tenderloin. Put them in a shallow bowl with the remaining oil, cover and put in a cool place until ready to cook.

If you don't use a lid and drip tray, move the coals so there are less on one side than the other. Move the pork frequently during cooking to prevent burning.

Prepare the barbecue. Twenty minutes before you are ready to cook, season the meat with salt. Wipe any excess oil off the meat. Once the flames have died down, rake the hot coals to one side and insert a drip tray flat beside them. Position a lightly oiled grill rack over the coals to heat.

When the coals are hot, or with a light coating of ash, put the tenderloins on to the grill rack over the coals. Grill for 5 minutes over the coals, turning to sear on all sides, then move them over the drip tray and grill for 15 minutes more. Cover with a lid or tented heavy-duty foil, and turn them over from time to time. When done, remove and wrap in foil. Leave to rest for 10 minutes before slicing into rounds and serving.

rempah rempah burgers

Makes 8

500g/1¼lb/2½ cups minced (ground) beef

5ml/1 tsp anchovy paste

10ml/2 tsp tomato purée (paste)

10ml/2 tsp ground coriander

5ml/1 tsp ground cumin

7.5ml/1½ tsp finely grated fresh root ginger

2 garlic cloves, crushed

1 egg white

75g/3oz solid creamed coconut or 40g/1½oz dessicated (dry unsweetened shredded) coconut

45ml/3 tbsp chopped fresh coriander (cilantro)

salt and ground black pepper

8 fresh vine leaves (optional), to serve

This recipe was given to me many years ago by a Malaysian friend living in Hong Kong, although the burgers are actually Indonesian. The coconut, which may seem unusual, actually gives the burgers a rich and succulent flavour. They taste great with a sharp yet sweet mango chutney and can be eaten in mini naan or pitta breads.

Mix the minced beef, anchovy paste, tomato purée, coriander, cumin, ginger and garlic in a bowl. Add the egg white, with salt and pepper to taste. Using your hands, mix well, making sure that the egg white is well amalgamated. Grate the block of coconut and work it gently into the meat mixture so that it doesn't melt, with the fresh coriander. Form into eight chunky burgers, about 7.5cm/3in in diameter. Chill for 30 minutes.

Prepare the barbecue. Once the flames have died down, rake the hot coals to one side and insert a drip tray flat beside them. Position a lightly oiled grill rack over the coals to heat. When the coals are medium-hot, or with a moderate coating of ash, place the chilled burgers on the rack over the drip tray. Cook for 10–15 minutes, turning them over once or twice. Check they are cooked by breaking off a piece of one of the burgers.

If you are using the vine leaves, wash them and pat dry with kitchen paper. Wrap one around each burger. Serve with the mango chutney and mini naan or pitta breads.

pandanus-flavoured chicken satay
with hot cashew nut sambal

Sometimes known as screwpine or bandan leaves, pandanus is common to Thai and South East Asian cooking. They are enormously versatile, and are used here for the delicate flavour they bring to the chicken as well as for their visual appeal. As the skewers cook, the aroma of the pandanus leaves are released, gently flavouring the chicken.

Serves 6

about 1kg/2¼lb skinless chicken breast fillets

30ml/2 tbsp olive oil

5ml/1 tsp ground coriander

2.5ml/½ tsp ground cumin

2.5cm/1in piece of fresh root ginger, finely grated

2 garlic cloves, crushed

5ml/1 tsp caster (superfine) sugar

2.5ml/½ tsp salt

18 long pandanus leaves, each halved to give 21cm/8½in lengths

36 long bamboo or wooden skewers

For the hot cashew nut sambal

2 garlic cloves, roughly chopped

4 small fresh hot green chillies (not tiny birdseye chillies), seeded and sliced

50g/2oz/⅓ cup cashew nuts

10ml/2 tsp sugar, preferably palm sugar

75ml/5 tbsp light soy sauce

juice of ½ lime

30ml/2 tbsp coconut cream

To make the sambal, place the garlic and chillies in a mortar and grind them quite finely with a pestle. Add the nuts and continue to grind until the mixture is almost smooth, with just a bit of texture. Pound in the remaining ingredients, cover and put in a cool place until needed.

Soak the bamboo or wooden skewers in water for 30 minutes. Slice the chicken horizontally into thin pieces and then into strips about 2.5cm/1in wide. Toss in the oil. Mix the coriander, cumin, ginger, garlic, sugar and salt together. Rub this mixture into the strips of chicken. Leave to marinate while you prepare the barbecue.

Thread a strip of pandanus leaf and a piece of chicken lengthways on to each skewer. Once the flames have died down, rake the coals to one side. Position a lightly oiled grill rack over the coals to heat.

A fast and efficient way of removing the seeds from small chillies is to cut off the stalk end, roll the chilli between your fingers, then bang it firmly against the sink; and the seeds will just drop out. If you like a very hot sambal, leave the seeds in the chillies.

When the coals are medium-hot to cool, or with a moderate to thick coating of ash, place the satays meat-side down over the coals and cover with a lid or tented heavy-duty foil and cook for 5–7 minutes. Once the meat has seared, move the satays around so that the leaves don't scorch. Serve, hot, with the sambal.

paprika-crusted monkfish
with chorizo and peppers

Such a chunky fish as monkfish is just perfect for skewering, as it is not likely to disintegrate before your eyes and fall between the grill bars as you cook. Monkfish can also take some fairly butch flavours, such as this smoky paprika crust, fruity charred red peppers and spicy chorizo. The brilliant whiteness of this fish when cut open makes a wonderful contrast to the red crust and the drizzle of palest green cucumber and mint sauce.

Serves 4

1 monkfish tail, about 1kg/2¼lb, trimmed and filleted

10ml/2 tsp smoked red paprika

2 red (bell) peppers, halved and seeded

15ml/1 tbsp extra virgin olive oil

16 thin slices of chorizo

salt and ground black pepper

4 long skewers

For the cucumber and mint sauce

150ml/¼ pint/⅔ cup Greek (US strained plain) yogurt

½ cucumber, halved lengthways and seeded

30ml/2 tbsp chopped fresh mint leaves

Place both monkfish fillets in a flat dish. Rub them all over with 5ml/1 tsp salt, then cover and leave in a cool place for 20 minutes. Pour the yogurt for the sauce into a food processor. Cut the cucumber into it, season with a little salt and pulse to a pale green purée. Transfer into a serving bowl and stir in the mint.

Prepare the barbecue. Rinse the salt off the pieces of monkfish and lightly pat them dry with kitchen paper. Mix the smoked red paprika with a pinch of salt and gently rub the mixture evenly over the fish. Slice each pepper into twelve long strips and cut each monkfish fillet into ten equal pieces. Thread six pieces of pepper and five pieces of fish on to each skewer and brush one side with a little extra virgin olive oil.

If it is easier, fry the chorizo on a hot griddle set on the grill rack for 30 seconds each side.

Once the flames have died down, position a lightly oiled grill rack over the coals to heat. When the coals are medium-hot, or with a moderate coating of ash, grill the skewered food, oiled-side down, for about 3½ minutes. Lightly brush the top side with oil, turn over and cook for 3–4 minutes more. Remove the skewers from the heat and keep warm. Grill the chorizo slices for a second or two until just warm.

Thread one piece on to the end of each skewer and serve the rest alongside on individual plates. Serve with the prepared cucumber and mint sauce.

seafood spiked on sugar cane
with tolee molee

Tolee molee are Burmese bits and pieces that accompany a main course. For this dish, bowls of herbs, crispy fried onions and balachaung, a wonderful chilli and prawn paste that comes in a jar, make ideal choices. They are easy to prepare but full of flavour. The sugar cane spikes make a great pick-up vehicle.

Makes 12

400g/14oz Mediterranean prawns (jumbo shrimp), peeled

225g/8oz skinned cod or halibut fillet, roughly cut into pieces

pinch of ground turmeric

1.5ml/¼ tsp ground white pepper

1.5ml/¼ tsp salt

60ml/4 tbsp chopped fresh coriander (cilantro)

1 fresh long red chilli, seeded and finely chopped

30ml/2 tbsp sunflower oil

a piece of sugar cane cut into 12 spikes or 12 wooden skewers

For the tolee molee

25g/1oz/½ cup coriander leaves

45ml/3 tbsp olive oil

300g/11oz sweet onions, halved and finely sliced

90ml/6 tbsp balachaung

15ml/1 tbsp sugar

juice of ½ lime

30ml/2 tbsp water

Soak the sugar cane spikes or wooden skewers in water for about 30 minutes. Make a shallow cut down the centre of the curved back of the prawn. Pull out the black vein with a cocktail stick (toothpick) or wipe out with kitchen paper. Slice the prawns roughly and place in a food processor with the fish, turmeric, pepper and salt. Pulse until the mixture forms a paste. Add the coriander and chilli and pulse lightly to combine with the other ingredients. Spoon into a bowl and chill for 30 minutes.

To make sugar cane spikes, chop through the length using a cook's knife and split into 1cm/½in shards. The sugar cane can be bought from ethnic grocers.

Make the tolee molee. Place the coriander leaves in a small serving bowl filled with cold water. Chill. Heat the olive oil in a large frying pan and fry the sliced onion over a medium heat for 10 minutes, stirring occasionally and increasing the heat for the last few minutes so that the onions become golden and crisp. Pile them into a serving bowl. Place the balachaung in a serving bowl. Mix the sugar, lime juice and measured water, stir into the balachaung and set aside.

Prepare the barbecue. Using damp hands, mould the seafood mixture around the drained sugarcane spikes or wooden skewers, so that it forms an oval sausage shape.

Once the flames have died down, position a lightly oiled grill rack over the coals to heat. When the coals are medium-hot, or with a moderate coating of ash, brush the seafood with the sunflower oil and grill for about 3 minutes each side until just cooked through. Serve with the tolee molee.

raffia-tied mackerel
with nutty bacon stuffing

This stuffed mackerel recipe was inspired by a popular Turkish dish called *uskumru dolmasi*. The mackerel are stuffed, tied with raffia and then grilled. They taste just as good cold so, when mackerel are at their peak, make extra for lunch next day and serve with horseradish mayonnaise and some peppery rocket.

Serves 6

45ml/3 tbsp olive oil

2 onions, finely chopped

2 garlic cloves, crushed

6 rindless smoked bacon rashers (strips), diced

50g/2oz/½ cup pine nuts

45ml/3 tbsp chopped fresh sweet marjoram

6 mackerel, about 300g/11oz each, cleaned but with heads left on

salt and ground black pepper

lemon wedges, to serve

raffia, soaked in water

Heat the oil in a large frying pan and sweat the chopped onions and garlic over a medium heat for 5 minutes. Increase the heat and add the bacon and pine nuts. Fry for a further 5–7 minutes, stirring occasionally, until golden. Tip into a bowl to cool. Gently fold in the sweet marjoram, season lightly, cover and chill until needed.

To prepare each fish, snip the backbone at the head end. Extend the cavity opening at the tail end so you can reach the backbone more easily. Turn the fish over and, with the heel of your hand, press firmly along the entire length of the backbone to loosen it. Snip the bone at the tail end and it will lift out surprisingly easily. Season the insides lightly.

If you are cooking these on a charcoal kettle barbecue, and the heat is too intense, reduce it a little by half-closing the air vents.

Stuff the cavity in each mackerel with some of the chilled onion mixture, then tie the mackerel along its entire length with raffia to hold in the stuffing. Chill the fish for at least 15 minutes. They can be chilled for up to 2 hours, but if so, allow them to come to room temperature for about 15 minutes before grilling.

Prepare the barbecue. Once the flames have died down, position a lightly oiled grill rack over the coals to heat. When the coals are medium-hot, or with a moderate coating of ash, transfer the mackerel to the grill rack and cook for about 8 minutes on each side, or until cooked and golden.

If your barbecue has a lid, use it. This will help you achieve an even golden skin without needing to move the fish about. Serve the mackerel with lemon wedges and black pepper.

patra ni macchi

This is a Parsi Indian gem, and the name means fish in a leaf parcel. I first ate it in Mumbai while being entertained by a merchant banker. Of his three chefs, one was dedicated solely to the cooking of local dishes. He used silver pomfret that tasted as if it had just leapt out of the Arabian sea into its banana leaf package. Here, salmon is used instead of pomfret; the gutsy flavours really work well.

Serves 6

50g/2oz fresh coconut, skinned and finely grated, or 65g/2½oz/scant 1 cup desiccated (dry unsweetened shredded) coconut, soaked in 30ml/2 tbsp water

1 large lemon, skin, pith and seeds removed, roughly chopped

4 large garlic cloves, crushed

3 large fresh mild green chillies, seeded and chopped

50g/2oz fresh coriander (cilantro), roughly chopped

25g/1oz fresh mint leaves, roughly chopped

5ml/1 tsp ground cumin

5ml/1 tsp sugar

2.5ml/½ tsp fenugreek seeds, finely ground

5ml/1 tsp salt

2 large, whole banana leaves

6 salmon fillets, total weight about 1.2kg/2½lb, skinned

Place all the ingredients except the banana leaves and salmon in a food processor. Pulse to a fine paste. Scrape the mixture into a bowl, cover and chill for 30 minutes.

Prepare the barbecue. While it is heating, make the parcels. Cut each banana leaf widthways into three and cut off the hard outside edge from each piece. Put the pieces of leaf and the edge strips in a bowl of hot water. Leave to soak for about 10 minutes. Drain, gently wipe off any white residue, rinse the leaves and strips, and pour over boiling water to soften. Drain, then place the leaves, smooth-side up, on a clean board.

Smear the top and bottom of each with the coconut paste. Place one fillet on each banana leaf. Bring the trimmed edge of the leaf over the salmon, then fold in the sides. Finally, bring up the remaining edge to cover the salmon and make a neat parcel. Tie each parcel securely with a leaf strip.

Lay each parcel on a sheet of heavy-duty foil, bring up the edges and scrunch the tops together to seal. Once the flames have died down, position a lightly oiled grill rack over the coals to heat. When the coals are medium-hot, or with a moderate coating of ash, place the salmon parcels on the grill rack and cook for about 10 minutes, turning over once.

Serve little rice parcels with the fish. Fill six more banana leaf packages with cooked basmati rice coloured with ground turmeric, secure each one with a skewer and reheat on the barbecue.

Place on individual plates and leave to stand for 2–3 minutes – the salmon will continue to cook for a bit in the residual heat of the parcel. Remove the foil, then carefully unwrap and eat the fish straight out of the parcel.

grilled nectarines
with amaretti morbidi and peach syllabub

This Italian dessert is highly addictive, with its irresistible syllabub flavoured with peach schnapps. The Italians have long known a thing or two about the delectable flavours that result from marrying fruit with almonds. Here, ripe nectarines are used, which look stunning slightly caramelized on top and decorated with grill marks.

Serves 8

120ml/4fl oz/½ cup peach schnapps

juice of ½ lemon

25g/1oz/¼ cup icing (confectioners') sugar

300ml/½ pint/1¼ cups double (heavy) cream

4 large ripe nectarines, halved and stoned

5ml/1 tsp clear honey

24 amaretti morbidi (soft almond macaroons)

Mix the peach schnapps, lemon juice and icing sugar in a large, deep bowl. Cover and chill.

Prepare the barbecue. Whisking constantly with a hand-held electric whisk, gradually add the cream to the chilled schnapps mixture, until the syllabub just holds its shape. Don't over whip. Chill the syllabub while you cook the fruit.

Brush each of the halved nectarines with a little honey. Once the flames have died down, position a lightly oiled grill rack over the coals to heat. When the coals are medium-hot, or with a moderate coating of ash, place the nectarines cut-side down on the grill rack and cook for about 1 minute.

These nectarines are easily cooked on the griddle, either on the barbecue or on the stovetop. Follow the timings given below.

Grill the amaretti morbidi for about 45 seconds on each side, to warm them through and let the surface caramelize a little. Serve the nectarines and amaretti with the syllabub.

give it time

give it time

this is how entertaining should be: prepare
everything beforehand, then relax on the day

There is something very satisfying about having done all the hard work in advance, knowing that all you have to do to complete a meal is put a little salsa together or transfer ready-to-cook brochettes from the refrigerator to the grill rack. When time is on your side, take the opportunity to steep basil in oil, make a bold aji amarillo marmalade or prepare a chilli-and-herb grilled polenta, then put aside to let the flavours improve and develop. Corn smeared with chipotle chilli butter and wrapped in its husk, or lamb in a rosemary-scented marinade will both benefit wonderfully from a few hours resting. While they do so, you can relax – safe in the knowledge that it will all taste and smell superb once it's sizzling away on the barbecue or griddle.

chilli-and-herb grilled polenta
with tangy pebre

Polenta has become as widely accepted as mashed potato and can confidently be classed as comfort food. Here it is flavoured with pasilla chillies, which have a dried fruit and slight liquorice hint to them. Serve it with a tangy salsa from Chile called pebre. This dish is especially good for a Sunday brunch teamed with crisp bacon.

Serves 6–12

10ml/2 tsp crushed dried pasilla chilli flakes

1.3 litres/2¼ pints/5⅔ cups water

250g/9oz/1¼ cups quick cook polenta

50g/2oz/¼ cup butter

75g/3oz Parmesan cheese, finely grated

30ml/2 tbsp chopped fresh dill

30ml/2 tbsp chopped fresh coriander (cilantro)

30ml/2 tbsp olive oil

salt

For the pebre

½ pink onion, finely chopped

4 drained bottled sweet cherry peppers, finely chopped

1 fresh medium hot red chilli, seeded and finely chopped

1 small red (bell) pepper, quartered and seeded

10ml/2 tsp raspberry vinegar

30ml/2 tbsp olive oil

4 tomatoes, halved, cored, seeded and roughly chopped

45ml/3 tbsp chopped fresh coriander (cilantro)

Chop the dried chilli flakes so that they are even finer. Put them in a pan with the water. Bring to the boil and add salt to taste. Pour the polenta into the water in a continuous stream, whisking all the time. Reduce the heat and continue to whisk for a few minutes. When the polenta is thick and bubbling like a volcano, whisk in the butter, Parmesan and herbs. Season with salt. Pour into a greased 33 x 23cm/ 13 x 9in baking tray and leave to cool. Leave uncovered so that the surface firms up and chill overnight.

About an hour before you plan to serve the meal, make the pebre. Place the onion, sweet cherry peppers and chilli in a mortar. Slice the skin from the red pepper quarters. Dice the flesh finely and add it to the mortar with the raspberry vinegar and olive oil. Pound with a pestle for about 1 minute, then tip into a serving dish. Stir in the tomatoes and coriander. Cover and leave in a cool place.

Remove the polenta from the refrigerator and leave for about 30 minutes. Cut into 12 even triangles and brush the top with oil. Heat a griddle until a few drops of water sprinkled on the surface evaporate instantly. Lower the heat to medium and grill the polenta triangles in batches oiled-side down for about 2 minutes, then turn through 180 degrees and cook for 1 minute more, to get a striking chequered effect. Serve the polenta at once, with the chilled pebre.

The polenta triangles can be cooked directly on an oiled grill rack on the barbecue if you prefer. Make sure they are well seared on one side before turning over to cook the other side.

whole stuffed squid on sticks

Preparing squid yourself may seem like a form of punishment, but it is the best way to ensure that the seafood is at its freshest. The process can even be rather therapeutic, but you can always ask the fishmonger to do it for you, if you prefer. The tentacles are a wonderfully tasty part of the squid so do skewer them as well.

Serves 6

12 whole squid, total weight about 675g/1½lb

45ml/3 tbsp extra virgin olive oil, plus extra for coating

2 onions, finely chopped

3 garlic cloves, crushed

25g/1oz/2 tbsp walnuts, finely chopped

7.5ml/1½ tsp ground sumac or squeeze of lemon juice

1.5ml/¼ tsp chilli flakes, finely chopped

75–90g/3–3½oz rocket (arugula), any tough stalks removed

115g/4oz/1 cup cooked rice

salt and ground black pepper

6 wooden or metal skewers

lemon and lime wedges, to serve

To prepare the squid, hold the body firmly in one hand and grasp the tentacles at their base with the other. Pull the head away from the body, bringing the entrails with it. Cut the tentacles (and part of the head above the eyes) away from the entrails. Snip out the hard beak in the middle of the clump of tentacles and discard this, along with the entrails attached to the remainder of the head. Peel the purplish membrane away from the body, then pull out the hard transparent quill and discard. Wash the clumps of tentacles and body well, inside and out, under cold running water.

Put the tentacles on a plate, cover and chill. Pull the side flaps or wings away from the body, chop them finely and set aside. Reserve the squid body with the tentacles.

Heat a frying pan. Add the oil, onions and garlic and fry for 5 minutes, or until the onions are soft and golden. Add the chopped squid wings and fry for about 1 minute, then stir in the walnuts, sumac and chilli flakes. Add the rocket and continue to stir-fry until it has wilted. Stir in the rice, season well and tip into a bowl to cool. If using wooden skewers, soak them in water for 30 minutes.

Prepare the barbecue. Stuff each squid with the cold mixture and thread two on to each skewer, with two clumps of tentacles. Toss in oil and salt. Once the flames have died down, position a lightly oiled grill rack over the coals to heat. When the coals are medium-hot, or with a moderate coating of ash, grill the squid for about 1½ minutes on each side. Once they are pale golden, move them to a cooler part of the grill to cook for 1½ minutes more on each side to ensure the filling is hot. Baste with any remaining oil and salt mixture as they are turned. Serve with lemon and lime wedges.

If you prepare these squid ahead of time, they can be chilled until needed. Remember to bring them back to room temperature before grilling.

husk-grilled corn on the cob

Keeping the husks on the corn protects the kernels and encloses the butter, so the flavours are contained. Fresh corn with husks intact are perfect, but banana leaves or a double layer of foil are also suitable.

Heat a heavy frying pan. Add the dried chillies and roast them by stirring them continuously for 1 minute without letting them scorch. Put them in a bowl with almost boiling water to cover. Use a saucer to keep them submerged, and leave them to rehydrate for up to 1 hour. Drain, remove the seeds and chop the chillies finely. Place the butter in a bowl and add the chillies, lemon juice and parsley. Season to taste and mix well.

Serves 6

3 dried chipotle chillies

250g/9oz/generous 1 cup butter, softened

7.5ml/1½ tsp lemon juice

45ml/3 tbsp chopped fresh flat leaf parsley

6 corn on the cob, with husks intact

salt and ground black pepper

Peel back the husks from each cob without tearing them. Remove the silk. Smear about 30ml/2 tbsp of the chilli butter over each cob. Pull the husks back over the cobs, ensuring that the butter is well hidden. Put the rest of the butter in a pot, smooth the top and chill to use later. Place the cobs in a bowl of cold water and leave in a cool place for 1–3 hours; longer if that suits your work plan better.

Prepare the barbecue. Remove the corn cobs from the water and wrap in pairs in foil. Once the flames have died down, position a lightly oiled grill rack over the coals to heat. When the coals are medium-hot, or have a moderate coating of ash, grill the corn for 15–20 minutes. Remove the foil and cook them for about 5 minutes more, turning them often to char the husks a little. Serve hot, with the rest of the butter.

hot avocado halves
with balsamic vinegar and basil oil

If you make the basil oil ahead of time, or buy a ready prepared basil oil, this is an ultra-simple dish that can be ready in a flash. It makes an eye-catching first course and is an excellent appetite teaser to serve while the rest of the food cooks on the barbecue.

Serves 6

3 ready-to-eat avocados, ideally Hass for flavour

105ml/7 tbsp balsamic vinegar

For the basil oil

40g/1½oz/1½ cups fresh basil leaves, stalks removed

200ml/7fl oz/scant 1 cup olive oil

To make the basil oil, place the leaves in a bowl and pour boiling water over. Leave for 30 seconds. Drain, refresh under cold water and drain again. Squeeze dry and pat with kitchen paper to remove as much moisture as possible. Place in a food processor with the oil and process to a purée. Put into a bowl, cover and chill overnight.

Line a sieve with muslin (cheesecloth), set it over a deep bowl and pour in the basil purée. Leave undisturbed for 1 hour, or until all the oil has filtered into the bowl. Discard the solids and pour into a bottle, then chill.

Prepare the barbecue. Cut each avocado in half and prize out the stone. Brush with a little of the oil. Heat the balsamic vinegar gently in a pan, on the stove or on the barbecue. When it starts to boil, simmer for 1 minute, or until it is just beginning to turn slightly syrupy.

Once the flames have died down, position a grill rack over the coals to heat. When the coals are hot, or with a light coating of ash, heat a griddle until a few drops of water sprinkled on to the surface evaporate instantly. Lower the heat a little, place the avocado halves cut-side down and cook for 30–60 seconds until branded with grill marks. Serve hot with the vinegar and extra oil drizzled over.

shish kebabs
with sumac and yogurt

Sumac is a spice, ground from a dried purple berry with a sour, fruity flavour. In this recipe it blissfully complements the richness of the lamb and yogurt. These kebabs are excellent served with little bowls of individual herbs dressed at the last minute with oil and lemon juice. The idea originated in Iran, where serving herbs at the end of the meal was believed to stop husbands' attention from straying.

Makes 8

675g/1½lb lamb neck (US shoulder or fillet) fillet, trimmed and cut into 2.5cm/1in pieces

5ml/1 tsp each fennel, cumin and coriander seeds, roasted and crushed

1.5ml/¼ tsp cayenne pepper

5cm/2in piece of fresh root ginger

150ml/¼ pint/⅔ cup Greek (US strained plain) yogurt

2 small red (bell) peppers

2 small yellow (bell) peppers

300g/11oz small or baby (pearl) onions

30ml/2 tbsp olive oil

15ml/1 tbsp ground sumac

salt and ground black pepper

8 long metal skewers

To serve

8 Lebanese flat breads

150ml/¼ pint/⅔ cup Greek (US strained plain) yogurt

5ml/1 tsp ground sumac

1 bunch rocket (arugula), about 50g/2oz

50g/2oz/2 cups fresh flat leaf parsley

10ml/2 tsp olive oil

juice of ½ lemon

Place the lamb pieces in a bowl and sprinkle over the crushed seeds and the cayenne pepper. Grate the ginger and squeeze it over the lamb. When all the juices have been extracted, discard the pulp. Pour over the yogurt. Mix well, cover and marinate overnight in the refrigerator.

Prepare the barbecue. Stand a large sieve over a bowl and pour in the lamb mixture. Leave to drain well. Cut the peppers in half, remove the cores and seeds, then cut the flesh into rough chunks. Place in a bowl. Add the onions and the olive oil. Pat the drained lamb with kitchen paper to remove excess marinade. Add the lamb to the bowl, season and toss well. Divide the lamb, peppers and onions into eight equal portions and thread on to the skewers. Do not pack them too tightly or they will not brown properly.

Once the flames have died down, position a lightly oiled grill rack over the coals to heat. When the coals are medium hot, or with a moderate coating of ash, grill the kebabs for about 10 minutes, turning every 2 minutes to prevent the meat and vegetables from getting too charred. When cooked, transfer the kebabs to a platter, lightly sprinkle with the sumac, cover loosely with foil, and leave to rest for a few minutes while you prepare the accompaniments.

If you want to use a griddle, cook the kebabs over a high heat to begin with, then lower the heat, and turn them frequently.

Wrap the breads in foil and put them on the barbecue to warm. Place the yogurt in a small serving bowl and sprinkle the surface with sumac. Arrange the rocket and parsley in separate bowls and pour over the oil and lemon juice. Serve with the kebabs and the warmed flat bread.

herb-flavoured butterflied leg of lamb

This boned leg of lamb is butterflied so that it cooks quickly on the barbecue, remaining tender and rare inside. Once the bone has been removed, cut into the thick parts of the meat to flatten it out. Rub the lamb with aniseed myrtle, a subtly flavoured Australian native herb.

Serves 6

1 leg of lamb, about 1.8kg/4lb, boned and butterflied

1 lemon

15ml/1 tbsp ground Australian aniseed myrtle or 5ml/1 tsp fennel seeds ground with 10ml/2 tsp dried thyme

90ml/6 tbsp extra virgin olive oil

salt and ground black pepper

3 long metal skewers

Lay the lamb in a flat dish. Squeeze the lemon juice over both sides of the meat, then season with pepper. Rub the myrtle or fennel and thyme, and the oil, over both sides of the meat. Cover and marinate in the refrigerator overnight. Remove it from the refrigerator 1½ hours before you start cooking. After 30 minutes, rub some salt all over the lamb.

Prepare the barbecue. Lift the lamb out of the marinade, and reserve the marinade. Pat the lamb dry with kitchen paper to remove all the excess marinade, then skewer the lamb in three places to keep it flat. Once the flames have died down, rake the hot coals to one side and insert a drip tray flat beside them. Position a lightly oiled grill rack over the coals to heat. When the coals are hot, or with a light coating of ash, lay the lamb on the grill rack over the coals for 3–5 minutes to lightly char one side. Turn the lamb over and put it back on the grill rack, this time over the drip tray. Cover with a lid or tented heavy-duty foil. Grill the lamb for 20 minutes, basting the charred side occasionally with the marinade to keep it moist.

Move the lamb so that it is over the coals, replace the lid and grill it for 5–8 minutes more so that it chars slightly. Lift it on to a tray and let it rest under tented foil for 10–15 minutes. Cut into thick slices and serve with the juices from the drip tray.

rosemary-scented frenched lamb

The best thing about this recipe is that all the work is done the night before. It used to be a regular treat whenever we were on holiday. While we drove, it would sit in its marinade jogging around in the back of the car, until a suitable picnic spot was found. The chargrilled lamb was absolute heaven with a bottle of red wine, salad, bread and cheese.

Serves 4–8

2 x 8-chop racks of lamb, French trimmed

8 large fresh rosemary sprigs

2 garlic cloves, thinly sliced

90ml/6 tbsp extra virgin olive oil

30ml/2 tbsp verjuice or red wine

salt and ground black pepper

Cut the racks into eight portions, each consisting of two linked chops, and tie a rosemary sprig to each one. Lay them in a single layer in a bowl. Mix the garlic, oil and verjuice or wine, and pour over the lamb, cover and chill overnight, turning them as often as possible.

Bring the lamb to room temperature 1 hour before cooking. Prepare the barbecue. Remove the lamb from the marinade, and discard the marinade. Season the meat 15 minutes before cooking. Once the flames have died down, position a lightly oiled grill rack over the coals to heat. When the coals are medium-hot, or with a moderate coating of ash, stand the lamb chops upright on the rack, propping them against each other. Cover with a lid or tented heavy-duty foil and grill for 2 minutes. Carefully turn on to one side, and grill for a further 4 minutes each side for rare meat or 5 minutes if you prefer lamb medium cooked.

Remove the chops from the grill, cover and rest for 5–10 minutes before serving.

barbecued bulgogi
with sigumchi namul and kimchi

Serves 4

500g/1¼lb beef fillet (tenderloin)

15ml/1 tbsp sugar

30ml/2 tbsp light soy sauce

30ml/2 tbsp sesame oil

2 garlic cloves, mashed to a paste with a further 5ml/1 tsp sugar

2.5ml/½ tsp finely ground black pepper

For the kimchi

500g/1¼lb Chinese leaves (Chinese cabbage), sliced across into 2.5cm/1in pieces

60ml/4 tbsp sunflower oil

15ml/1 tbsp sesame oil

50g/2oz/¼ cup sugar

105ml/7 tbsp white rice vinegar

2.5cm/1in piece of fresh root ginger, finely chopped

3 garlic cloves, finely chopped

1 fresh fat medium hot red chilli

2 spring onions (scallions), thinly sliced

For the sigumchi namul

350g/12oz baby spinach leaves

10ml/2 tsp sesame oil

30ml/2 tbsp light soy sauce

15ml/1 tbsp mirin

10ml/2 tsp sesame seeds, finely toasted

I first ate this marinated beef dish in a small Korean barbecue restaurant tucked away in the basement of the Hyatt Regency in Hong Kong. The atmosphere inside was so smoky that the venue could only be visited on hair-washing nights. Bulgogi is served here with bowls of sigumchi namul – a mix of spinach, sesame oil and seeds – and my version of kimchi, which, unlike the original Korean cabbage dish, does not need to be fermented first in an earth pit.

Freeze the beef for 1 hour to make it easier to slice. Remove it from the freezer and slice it as thinly as possible. Layer in a shallow dish, sprinkling each layer with sugar. Cover and chill for 30 minutes. Mix the soy sauce, sesame oil, garlic paste and pepper together in a bowl and pour over the beef, ensuring all the pieces are thoroughly coated in the mixture. Cover and chill overnight.

To make the kimchi, blanch the Chinese leaves in plenty of boiling water for 5 seconds, drain and refresh under cold running water. Drain again and pat with kitchen paper to remove excess water. Put the Chinese leaves in a bowl. Mix the remaining ingredients together and add to the leaves. Toss to mix, cover and chill. The mixture can be made up to 2 days ahead, but tastes best if eaten within 2 hours.

Bulgogi is best cooked on a close-meshed disposable barbecue as the meat may fall through the gaps in grill racks of other barbecues. You can, however, use the griddle on the barbecue over very hot coals.

To make the sigumchi namul, blanch the spinach in boiling water for 1 minute, drain it and refresh under cold water. Drain again, pat with kitchen paper to remove any excess water and put into a serving bowl. Mix the oil, soy sauce and mirin together. Fold into the spinach, with the sesame seeds. Cover and keep in a cool place (not the refrigerator). Serve within 2 hours.

Heat a griddle on the stove over a high heat until a few drops of water sprinkled on to the surface evaporate instantly. Flash-fry the meat in batches for 15–20 seconds on each side. Serve immediately with the sigumchi namul and the kimchi.

sichuan pork ribs
with ginger and shallot relish

This dish has slowly evolved from a recipe given to me years ago. It works best when the pork ribs are grilled in whole, large slabs, then sliced to serve. Not only does this keep the meat succulent, but there is also no better way to get everyone hankering for a juicy rib to chew.

Serves 4

4 pork rib slabs, each with 6 ribs, total weight about 2kg/4½lb

40g/1½oz/3 tbsp light muscovado sugar

3 garlic cloves, crushed

5cm/2in piece of fresh root ginger, finely grated

10ml/2 tsp Sichuan peppercorns, finely crushed

2.5ml/½ tsp ground black pepper

5ml/1 tsp finely ground star anise

5ml/1 tsp Chinese five-spice powder

90ml/6 tbsp dark soy sauce

45ml/3 tbsp sunflower oil

15ml/1 tbsp sesame oil

For the relish

60ml/4 tbsp sunflower oil

300g/11oz banana shallots, finely chopped

9 garlic cloves, crushed

7.5cm/3in piece of fresh root ginger, finely grated

60ml/4 tbsp seasoned rice wine vinegar

45ml/3 tbsp sweet chilli sauce

105ml/7 tbsp tomato ketchup

90ml/6 tbsp water

60ml/4 tbsp chopped fresh coriander (cilantro) leaves

salt

Lay the slabs of pork ribs in a large shallow dish. Mix the remaining ingredients in a bowl and pour the marinade over the ribs, making sure they are evenly coated. Cover and chill the ribs overnight.

Make the relish. This can be made the day before you intend to serve it, if you like. Heat the oil in a heavy pan, add the shallots and cook them gently for 5 minutes. Add the garlic and ginger and cook for about 4 minutes more. Increase the heat and add all the remaining ingredients except the coriander. Cover and simmer gently for 10 minutes until thickened. Tip into a bowl and stir in the coriander. When completely cold, chill until needed.

Remove the ribs from the refrigerator 1 hour before cooking. Prepare the barbecue. Remove the ribs from the marinade and pat them dry with kitchen paper. Pour the marinade into a pan. Bring it to the boil on the stove, then lower the heat and simmer for 3 minutes.

Once the flames have died down, carefully rake the hot coals to one side and insert a large drip tray flat beside them. Position a lightly oiled grill rack over the coals to heat. When the coals are hot, or with a light coating of ash, lay the ribs over the coals and cook them for 3 minutes on each side, then move over the drip tray. Cover with a lid or tented heavy-duty foil and cook for a further 30–35 minutes, turning and basting occasionally with the marinade, until the meat is tender and golden brown all over.

Banana shallots are a welcome relief when it comes to onion chopping. Their torpedo shape makes them easy to peel and chop.

If the ribs need crisping up due to the frequent basting, move them quickly back over the coals. Stop basting with the marinade 5 minutes before cooking time. Cut into single ribs to serve, with the relish.

mini chicken fillets
with aji amarillo marmalade

The aji amarillo is a yellowy orange Peruvian chilli, very fruity and quite hot, which is why it is a good idea to prepare the marmalade the day before so that the flavours can mellow and blend. The chicken fillets are steeped in oil and garlic before being grilled really quickly. They are great when served with the marmalade and lightly charred flat bread.

Serves 4

500g/1¼lb mini chicken breast fillets or skinless chicken breast fillets, each cut into 4 long strips

2 garlic cloves, crushed to a paste with 2.5ml/½ tsp salt

30ml/2 tbsp olive oil

ground black pepper

For the aji amarillo marmalade

50g/2oz dried aji amarillo chillies

120ml/4fl oz/½ cup water

20ml/4 tsp olive oil

2 onions, finely chopped

3 garlic cloves, crushed

5ml/1 tsp ground cumin

10ml/2 tsp Mexican oregano

130g/4½oz/scant ¾ cup sugar

200ml/7fl oz/scant 1 cup cider or white wine vinegar

2 small orange (bell) peppers, quartered and seeded

Make the aji amarillo marmalade. Heat a heavy frying pan, add the dried chillies and roast them by stirring them continuously over the heat for about 1½ minutes without letting them scorch. Put them in a bowl with just enough almost boiling water to cover. Use a saucer to keep them submerged and leave to rehydrate for about 2 hours, or longer if you prefer.

Slit the chillies, remove the seeds and chop the flesh into small dice. Place in a food processor, add the water and process to a purée. Heat the oil in a heavy pan, add the onions and garlic and cook over a gentle heat for 5 minutes. Add the cumin, Mexican oregano and the chilli purée. Add the sugar and stir until turning syrupy, then add the vinegar and stir well. Bring the mixture to the boil, then lower the heat and simmer for 30 minutes.

Meanwhile, heat a griddle until a few drops of water sprinkled on the surface evaporate instantly. Roast the peppers, placed with skin-side down so that the skins char. Put the peppers into a bowl and cover tightly with clear film (plastic wrap). When they are cool enough to handle, rub off the skin and finely dice the flesh. Add to the chilli mixture and continue to simmer for about 25 minutes, or until the marmalade thickens. Transfer to a bowl. When cool, cover and chill until 30 minutes before serving.

The aji amarillo marmalade will keep, chilled, for a week. It is also good eaten with hot smoked salmon.

Spread out the chicken pieces in a shallow dish and add the garlic, oil and pepper. Turn the fillets in the mixture, cover and set aside in a cool place for 30–45 minutes, turning occasionally.

Prepare the barbecue. Once the flames have died down, position a lightly oiled grill rack over the coals to heat. When the coals are medium-hot, and with a moderate covering of ash, grill the chicken pieces for 2½–3 minutes on each side, or until cooked through and branded with grill marks. Move the food while cooking to avoid over-charring. Transfer to a platter, cover and leave in a warm place for 5 minutes before serving with the marmalade.

tandoori drumsticks
with kachumbar

No self-respecting book on grilling could leave out a tandoori dish – in this case, served with a chilli onion salad. When making kachumbar, use the pink onions available in West Indian markets if you can, but white sweet Italian ones would do. The onions are salted to extract the bitter juices, then mixed with chillies and ginger.

Serves 6

12 small chicken drumsticks, skinned

3 garlic cloves, crushed to a paste with a pinch of salt

150ml/¼ pint/⅔ cup Greek (US strained plain) yogurt

10ml/2 tsp ground coriander

5ml/1 tsp ground cumin

5ml/1 tsp ground turmeric

1.5ml/¼ tsp cayenne pepper

2.5ml/½ tsp garam masala

15ml/1 tbsp curry paste

juice of ½ lemon

salt

warmed naan breads, to serve

For the kachumbar

2 pink onions, halved and thinly sliced

10ml/2 tsp salt

4cm/1½in piece of fresh root ginger, finely shredded

2 fresh long green chillies, seeded and finely chopped

20ml/4 tsp sugar, preferably palm sugar

juice of ½ lemon

60ml/4 tbsp chopped fresh coriander (cilantro)

Using a sharp knife, score each drumstick around the flesh that attaches itself to the tip of the bone. This will make it easier to remove the end of the chunky knuckle after marinating. Place the drumsticks in a non-metallic bowl. Put the garlic, yogurt, spices, curry paste and lemon juice in a food processor and whizz until smooth. Pour the mixture over the drumsticks to coat, cover and chill overnight.

Two hours before serving make the kachumbar. Put the onion slices in a bowl, sprinkle them with the salt, cover and leave to stand for 1 hour. Tip into a sieve, rinse well under cold running water, then drain and pat dry. Roughly chop the slices and put them in a serving bowl. Add the remaining ingredients and mix well. About an hour before cooking, drain the drumsticks in a sieve set over a bowl. Remove the wobbly knuckle bone at the end of each drumstick with a sharp knife and scrape the flesh down a little to make the bone look clean. Return the drumsticks to the bowl of marinade.

The chunky knuckle end is softened by the marinade, which makes its removal easy.

Prepare the barbecue. About 30 minutes before you are ready to cook, salt the drumsticks. Once the flames have died down, position a lightly oiled grill rack over the coals to heat. When the coals are medium-hot, or with a moderate coating of ash, carefully lift the drumsticks out of the marinade. Wrap the tips with strips of foil to prevent them from burning, then place on the grill rack so that they are not directly over the coals. Cover with a lid or tented heavy-duty foil and grill for 5 minutes, turning frequently. Brush the drumsticks with a little of the marinade and cook for 5–7 minutes more, or until cooked. Serve hot with the kachumbar and naan breads.

mahi-mahi brochettes
with grill-roasted peperonata

Serves 4

8 fresh sprigs of bay leaves

**675g/1½lb mahi-mahi,
swordfish or marlin
fillet, skinned**

1 lime, halved

1 lemon, halved

60ml/4 tbsp olive oil

1 small garlic clove, crushed

**salt and ground
black pepper**

8 short wooden skewers

For the peperonata

**2 large red (bell) peppers,
quartered and seeded**

**2 large yellow (bell) peppers,
quartered and seeded**

**90ml/6 tbsp extra virgin
olive oil**

**2 sweet onions,
thinly sliced**

1 garlic clove, thinly sliced

5ml/1 tsp sugar

**4 tomatoes, peeled, seeded
and roughly chopped**

2 bay leaves

1 large fresh thyme sprig

**15ml/1 tbsp red verjuice or
red wine**

Peperonata was made popular as far back as the 1970s. In this dish, the peppers are roasted and skinned, giving the peperonata a lovely smoky flavour and smooth texture, while the verjuice, an unfermented grape juice, adds an underlying tartness. The fish brochettes make the perfect accompaniment, with their strong flavours. Mahi-mahi is an oily fish also known as llampuga, dorado or dolphin fish (no relation to the dolphin).

Make the peperonata. Spread out the pepper pieces on a board and brush the skin side with a little oil. Heat the remaining oil in a pan and add the onions and garlic. Fry over a medium-high heat for 6–8 minutes until lightly golden.

Heat a griddle until a few drops of water sprinkled on the surface evaporate instantly. Add the peppers, skin-side down. Lower the heat a little and grill them for 5 minutes until the skins are charred. Put them into a bowl and cover tightly with clear film (plastic wrap). When cool enough to handle, rub off the skins and slice each piece into six or seven strips. Add to the onion mixture, stir in the sugar and cook over a medium heat for about 2 minutes. Add the tomatoes and herbs and bring to the boil. Lower the heat, stir in the verjuice or wine, and simmer, uncovered, for about 30 minutes.

Soak the wooden skewers with the bay leaf sprigs in a bowl of cold water for 30 minutes. Cut the mahi-mahi into 12 large cubes and place in a bowl. Squeeze the juice from half a lime and half a lemon into a small bowl. Whisk in 45ml/3 tbsp of the oil. Cream the garlic and plenty of seasoning to a paste, add to the oil mixture and pour over the mahi-mahi. Marinate for 30 minutes.

The brochettes can also be cooked on an oiled grill rack over a medium to high heat. Follow the timings given below.

Drain the skewers and the bay leaves. Cut the remaining lime and lemon halves into four wedges each. Using two skewers placed side by side instead of the usual one, thread alternately with three pieces of fish, one lime and one lemon wedge and two sprigs of bay leaves. Make three more brochettes in the same way.

Replace the griddle over a high heat and test that it is hot. Brush the brochettes with the remaining oil and grill for 3–4 minutes on each side, or until the fish is cooked through and nicely branded. Cover and keep warm for up to 5 minutes before serving with the peperonata.

barbecued red snapper
in a banana leaf package

The red snapper is a line-caught reef fish from the Indian ocean and the Caribbean, beautiful to look at but with vicious spines and a fairly impenetrable armour of scales. Perhaps best if you ask the fishmonger to scale it. Leave the fins on, however, so that it retains its lovely fish-like quality.

Make the dipping sauce by mixing together the chilli, lime juice, fish sauce, sugar and water in a bowl. Cover and chill until needed.

Soak the wooden skewers in cold water for 30 minutes. Make four slashes in either side of each fish and rub the skin with oil.

Place half the ginger, shallots and the garlic in a mortar. Add half the sugar, the thinly sliced lemon grass, a little of the lime juice, the salt and the chillies and pound to break up and bruise. Mix in the remaining sugar and lime juice, with the lime rind. Rub a little of the mixture into the slashes and the bulk of it into the cavity of each fish.

Trim the hard edge from each banana leaf and discard it. Soak the banana leaves in hot water for 10 minutes, then drain. Wipe any white residue from the leaves. Rinse, then pour over boiling water to soften. Drain again. Lay a fish on each leaf and scatter the remaining ginger and shallots over them. Split the whole lemon grass stalks lengthways and lay the pieces over each fish. Bring the sides of the leaves up over the fish and secure using three wooden skewers for each envelope. Wrap in clear film (plastic wrap) to keep the wooden skewers moist, and chill for at least 30 minutes, but no more than 6 hours.

Prepare the barbecue. Bring the dipping sauce to room temperature. Remove the clear film from each banana leaf envelope and place each on a sheet of foil. Bring the sides of the foil up around each envelope to enclose it loosely. This will protect the base of each banana leaf wrapper.

Once the flames have died down, position a lightly oiled grill rack over the coals to heat. When the coals are medium-hot, or with a moderate coating of ash, lay the envelopes on the grill rack and cook for 15 minutes. Turn the envelopes around 180 degrees and cook for about 10 minutes more. Open up the foil for the last 5 minutes. Leave to stand for a further 5 minutes, then check to see if the fish is cooked by inserting a skewer – it should flake easily. Place on a large serving dish, open the envelopes and sprinkle the fish with the coriander. Serve with individual bowls and the sauce.

Serves 4

2 red snapper, each about 900g/2lb, cleaned and scaled, or tilapia

15ml/1 tbsp olive oil

5cm/2in piece of fresh root ginger, thinly sliced

4 banana shallots, total weight about 150g/5oz, thinly sliced

3 garlic cloves, thinly sliced

30ml/2 tbsp sugar

3 lemon grass stalks, 1 thinly sliced

grated rind and juice of 1 lime

5ml/1 tsp salt

4 small fresh green or red chillies, thinly sliced

2 whole banana leaves

30ml/2 tbsp chopped fresh coriander (cilantro)

6 wooden skewers

For the dipping sauce

1 large fresh red chilli, seeded and finely chopped

juice of 2 limes

30ml/2 tbsp fish sauce

5ml/1 tsp sugar

60ml/4 tbsp water

Serve leaf-wrapped rice parcels with the fish. Heat them up in foil next to the fish for the last 5 minutes. They can be found in larger Asian food stores.

vine-leaf-wrapped sea bass
stuffed with black rice

This dish is effortless but must be started in advance as the rice needs to be cold before it is used in the little parcels. Once the fish have been wrapped, all you have to do is keep them chilled, ready to pop on to the barbecue.

Serves 8 as a first course; 4 as a main course

90g/3½oz/½ cup Chinese black rice

400ml/14fl oz/1⅔ cups boiling water

45ml/3 tbsp extra virgin olive oil

1 small onion, chopped

1 fresh mild chilli, seeded and finely chopped

8 sea bass fillets, about 75g/3oz each, with skin

16 large fresh vine leaves

salt and ground black pepper

Place the rice in a large pan. Add the boiling water and simmer for 15 minutes. Add a little salt to taste and simmer for a further 10 minutes, or until tender. Drain well and tip into a bowl.

Meanwhile, heat half the oil in a frying pan. Fry the onion gently for 5 minutes until softened. Add the chilli. Stir into the rice mixture, adjust the seasoning and cool. Cover and chill until needed.

Season the sea bass fillets. Wash the vine leaves in water, then pat dry with kitchen paper. Lay each leaf in the centre of a double layer of foil. Top with a sea bass fillet. Divide the rice mixture among the fillets, spooning it towards one end. Fold the fillet over the rice, trickle over the remaining oil, lay the second vine leaf on top and bring the foil up around the fish and scrunch it together to seal. Chill the packages for up to 3 hours, or until needed.

Take the fish out of the refrigerator and prepare the barbecue. Once the flames have died down, position a lightly oiled grill rack over the coals to heat. When the coals are hot, or with a light coating of ash, place the parcels on the edge of the grill rack. Cook for 5 minutes, turning them around 90 degrees halfway through. Open up the top of the foil a little and cook for 2 minutes more. Gently remove from the foil and transfer the vine parcels to individual plates and serve.

For a quick salsa, chop half a seeded cucumber and half a pink onion. Place in a bowl and add 30ml/2 tbsp seasoned sushi vinegar and mix well. Add a little chilli to add a little kick to it.

grilled mango cheeks
with lime syrup and sorbet

If you can locate them, use Alphonso mangoes. Mainly cultivated in India, they have a heady scent and gloriously sensual, silky texture, which is balanced by the tart lime sorbet and syrup. They ripen in early summer and are available from specialist greengrocers.

Serves 6

250g/9oz/1¼ cups sugar

juice of 6 limes

3 star anise

6 small or 3 medium to large mangoes

groundnut (peanut) oil, for brushing

Place the sugar in a heavy pan and add 250ml/8fl oz/1 cup water. Heat gently until the sugar has dissolved. Increase the heat and boil for 5 minutes. Cool completely. Add the lime juice and any pulp that has collected in the squeezer. Strain the mixture and reserve 200ml/7fl oz/scant 1 cup in a bowl with the star anise.

Pour the remaining liquid into a measuring jug or cup and make up to 600ml/1 pint/2½ cups with cold water. Mix well and pour into a freezerproof container. Freeze for 1½ hours, stir well and return to the freezer for another hour until set.

Transfer the sorbet mixture to a processor and pulse to a smooth icy purée. Freeze for another hour or longer, if wished. Alternatively, make the sorbet in an ice cream maker; it will take about 20 minutes, and should then be frozen for at least 30 minutes before serving.

Pour the reserved syrup into a pan and boil for 2–3 minutes, or until thickened a little. Leave to cool. Cut the cheeks from either side of the stone on each unpeeled mango, and score the flesh on each in a diamond pattern. Brush with a little oil. Heat a griddle, until very hot and a few drops of water sprinkled on the surface evaporate instantly. Lower the heat a little and grill the mango halves, cut-side down, for 30–60 seconds until branded with golden grill marks.

If this dessert is part of a larger barbecue meal, cook the mangoes in advance using a griddle set over the first red hot coals. Set aside until ready, and serve cold.

Invert the mango cheeks on individual plates and serve hot or cold with the syrup drizzled over and a scoop or two of sorbet. Decorate with the reserved star anise.

make it an event

make it an event

these recipes are not just for the occasional
indulgence, though they do deserve a crowd

This is food for fun, to enjoy and impress. Ingredients are sometimes extravagant, but they may also be as simple as grilled sausages. Occasionally it is the setting that is just as much the star attraction as the dishes, as when lobster is served by the pool or damper skewers are cooked over the fire on the beach. The cockle and seafood bake is not something for under the pier at any holiday hot spot, but suggests a hidden cove with pebbles, seaweed and tinder-dry flotsam. A trip too far? Set the scene with silver sand and stones from the garden centre, arranged in an old steel wheelbarrow, then order the seaweed and seafood from the fishmonger.

Serves 8

500g/1¼lb/5 cups plain (all-purpose) flour

25ml/1½ tbsp baking powder

250g/9oz/1 cup plus 30ml/2 tbsp butter

30ml/2 tbsp chopped fresh rosemary, plus 1 sprig to flavour and use as a brush for the butter

1 large pinch of saffron threads mixed with 15ml/1 tbsp boiling water

175ml/6fl oz/¾ cup milk

salt

24 rosemary spikes or wooden skewers (or 12 of each)

damper skewers

This Antipodean's fireside favourite is also a bit of a Girl Guide tradition. It's a fun thing for a long, lazy beach barbecue. It is usual to cook damper in the embers of the fire, but rosemary skewers are a stylish alternative. Dunk the damper in tomato soup for a delicious meal.

Soak the rosemary spikes or wooden skewers in cold water for 30 minutes. Sift the flour, baking powder and salt into a large bowl. Rub in 200g/7oz/scant 1 cup of the butter until the mixture looks like fine breadcrumbs, then add the chopped rosemary. Strain the saffron water into the milk and add to the flour mixture all in one go. Mix to a paste with your hands and knead until the dough is smooth and elastic. Melt the remaining butter and stir it with the rosemary brush to infuse it with the flavour.

Prepare the barbecue. Drain the skewers or rosemary spikes. Divide the dough into 24 equal pieces and twist one piece around each skewer or spike. Once the flames have died down, position a lightly oiled grill rack over the coals to heat. When the coals are medium-hot, or with a moderate coating of ash, grill the spiked dough for 5 minutes, turning often, until cooked and golden. Brush occasionally with the rosemary dipped in butter and serve hot.

grilled baby artichokes

This is an enjoyable way to eat artichokes. Just hold the skewer with the artichoke in one hand, tear off a leaf with the other and dip that into the hot melted butter. It is important to use baby artichokes so that no one has to tussle with a hairy choke.

Serves 6

12 baby artichokes with stalks, total weight about 1.3kg/3lb

1 lemon, halved

200g/7oz/scant 1 cup butter

2 garlic cloves, crushed with a pinch of salt

15ml/1 tbsp flat leaf parsley

salt and ground black pepper

12 long wooden skewers

Soak the skewers in cold water for 30 minutes. Drain, then skewer a baby artichoke on each one. Bring a large pan of salted water to the boil. Squeeze the juice of one lemon half, and add it, with the lemon shell, to the pan. Place the artichokes head first into the pan and boil for 5–8 minutes, or until just tender. Drain well. Set aside for up to 1 hour or use at once.

Prepare the barbecue. Put the butter, garlic and parsley into a small pan and squeeze in the juice of the remaining lemon.

Once the flames have died down, position a lightly oiled grill rack over the coals to heat. When the coals are cool, or with a thick coating of ash, they are ready to cook the artichokes. If the artichokes have been allowed to cool, wrap the heads in heavy foil and place them on the grill for 3 minutes, then unwrap and return to the heat for 1 minute, turning frequently. If they are still hot, grill without the foil for 4 minutes, turning often.

When the artichokes are almost ready, melt the butter sauce in the pan on the barbecue. Serve it with the artichokes on their skewers.

marinated octopus on sticks
with red pipian

Octopus that is frozen and then thawed becomes tender in the process, and so it cooks quickly. Check with the fishmonger before buying, as fresh octopus will need considerably more simmering time. The red pipian is a simplified version of a Colombian pesto-like sauce. It is combined with ancho chilli, which is sweet and hot with a fruity fragrance when cooked.

Serves 8

1kg/2¼lb whole octopus

1 onion, quartered

2 bay leaves

30ml/2 tbsp olive oil

grated rind and juice of 1 lemon

15ml/1 tbsp chopped fresh coriander (cilantro)

8 metal skewers

For the red pipian

1 ancho chilli (dried poblano)

4 whole garlic cloves, peeled

1 small pink onion, chopped

500g/1¼lb plum tomatoes, cored and seeded

30ml/2 tbsp olive oil

5ml/1 tsp sugar

30ml/2 tbsp pine nuts

30ml/2 tbsp pumpkin seeds

pinch of ground cinnamon

15ml/1 tbsp chipotles in adobo or other sweet and smoky chilli sauce

45ml/3 tbsp vegetable stock

leaves from 4 large fresh thyme sprigs, finely chopped

salt

fresh coriander (cilantro) sprigs, to garnish

Make the red pipian. Preheat the oven to 200°C/400°F/Gas 6. Put the ancho chilli in a bowl and cover with water that has just gone off the boil. Leave to soak for about 20 minutes. Meanwhile place the garlic cloves, onion and tomatoes in a roasting pan and drizzle with the oil, sprinkle the sugar and a little salt over the top. Roast for 15 minutes. Add the pine nuts, pumpkin seeds and cinnamon to the top of the mixture and roast for a further 5 minutes. Meanwhile, drain the ancho chilli, remove the seeds and chop the flesh.

Transfer the roasted mixture and the ancho chilli to a food processor along with the chipotles in adobo or chilli sauce, vegetable stock and thyme. Pulse to a purée, then scrape into a serving bowl and leave to cool.

Trim the tentacles from the head of the octopus. Leave the skin on, but trim any large flaps with kitchen scissors. Discard the head. Place the tentacles in a large pan, cover with cold water and add the onion and bay leaves. Bring slowly to the boil, lower the heat and simmer for about 20 minutes if prefrozen, and up to 2 hours if fresh.

Drain the tentacles and rinse under cold water, rubbing off any loose dark membrane. Thread the tentacles on to the skewers and put in a plastic bag with the olive oil, lemon rind and juice, and chopped coriander. Tie shut and shake to mix. Leave to marinate in a cool place for at least 1 hour or up to 12 hours.

Prepare the barbecue. Once the flames have died down, position a lightly oiled grill rack over the coals to heat. When the coals are medium-hot, or with a moderate coating of ash, grill the octopus skewers for 2–4 minutes each side, or until nicely golden. Serve with the red pipian, garnished with the coriander sprigs.

Cook the skewered octopus on a griddle if you prefer, either over the coals or on the stovetop. The timing will be the same.

Serves 4

15g/½oz dried arame seaweed, rinsed in water

60ml/4 tbsp tamari

30ml/2 tbsp mirin

120ml/4fl oz/½ cup water

5ml/1 tsp white sesame seeds

250g/9oz sashimi tuna

15ml/1 tbsp black sesame seeds

10ml/2 tsp dried pink peppercorns

2.5ml/½ tsp sunflower oil

16 fresh shiso leaves

7.5ml/1½ tsp wasabi paste

50g/2oz finely grated mooli (daikon)

chargrilled tuna on shiso leaves
with wasabi and arame

Use sashimi-quality tuna from a Japanese food store or first-rate fishmonger, who will trim it to a neat rectangular shape. Shiso leaves, also knows as parilla, are related to basil and mint. They have a pungent flavour, a little like anise, and taste wonderful when wrapped around the tuna.

Drain the arame, then soak it in the tamari, mirin and water for 1 hour.

Pour the liquid from the arame into a small pan and put the arame in a serving bowl. Bring the liquid to a simmer. Cook for 3–5 minutes, or until syrupy, cool for 2 minutes and pour over the arami. Scatter with the white sesame seeds and cover until needed.

Place the tuna in a flat freezerproof container. Lightly grind the black sesame seeds and pink peppercorns in a spice mill. Brush the oil over the tuna, then roll the tuna into the spice mixture to coat it evenly. Heat a griddle until it is fiercely hot and smoking slightly. Sear the tuna for 30 seconds on each of the four sides. Put it back in its container and freeze for 5 minutes to stop it cooking any further. Slice it into 5mm/¼in wide pieces and arrange on plates with the shiso leaves, a blob of wasabi and a mound each of arame and mooli.

grilled foie gras
with asian pear and ponzu joyu

The rich and luxurious texture of the foie gras is teamed here with a sharp, tangy Japanese sauce, ponzu joyu. It takes only seconds to prepare but does need to be made at least 24 hours in advance to give the flavours plenty of time to blend. The caramelized flavour of the Asian pear balances the dish perfectly.

To make the ponzu joyu, place the mirin in a small pan, bring to the boil and cook for about 30 seconds. Pour into a small bowl and add all the remaining ingredients. Cool, then cover and chill for about 24 hours. Strain the mixture into a screw-topped jar and chill until needed.

Cut each pear into eight wedges and toss in the honey mixture. Heat a griddle on the stove until a drop of water sprinkled on the surface evaporates instantly. Grill the pear wedges for about 30 seconds on each cut side, or until branded with golden grill marks. Wipe the pan with kitchen paper and heat again. When it is searing hot, grill the foie gras for 30 seconds on each side. Serve immediately with the ponzu joyu and pear wedges.

This can also be cooked on a griddle on the barbecue over hot coals that have a light covering of ash.

Serves 4
2 Asian (nashi) pears

15ml/1 tbsp clear honey mixed with 45ml/ 3 tbsp water

225g/8oz duck or goose foie gras, chilled and cut into eight 1cm/½in slices

For the ponzu joyu
45ml/3 tbsp mirin

120ml/4fl oz/½ cup tamari

75ml/5 tbsp dried bonito flakes

45ml/3 tbsp rice vinegar

juice of 1 large lemon

4 strips dried kombu seaweed

vegetables in ashes
with smoked tomato salsa

Use a double layer of coals to start the barbecue so they will be deep enough to make a bed for the foil-wrapped vegetables. While these are cooking, make the smoked tomato salsa on the grill rack above.

Serves 4–6

2 small whole heads of garlic

2 butternut squash, about 450g/1lb each, halved lengthways and seeded

4–6 onions, about 115g/4oz each, with a cross cut in the top of each

4–6 baking potatoes, about 175g/6oz each

4–6 sweet potatoes, about 175g/6oz each

45ml/3 tbsp olive oil

fresh thyme, bay leaf and rosemary sprigs

salt and ground black pepper

2 handfuls of hickory wood chips soaked in cold water for at least 30 minutes

For the tomato salsa

500g/1¼lb tomatoes, quartered and seeded

2.5ml/½ tsp sugar

a pinch of chilli flakes

1.5ml/¼ tsp smoky sweet chilli powder

30ml/2 tbsp good quality tomato chutney

Prepare a barbecue with plenty of coals. Wrap the garlic, squash and onions separately in a double layer of heavy-duty foil, leaving them open. Wrap the potatoes in pairs, with one sweet and one ordinary potato. Drizzle a little oil over the contents of each packet, season well and pop in a herb sprig. Spray with a little water and scrunch up the foil to secure the parcels.

Once the flames have died down and the coals are hot, or with a light coating of ash, place the parcels on top of them, noting what goes where, if possible. The garlic will take 20 minutes to cook, the squash 30 minutes, the onions 45 minutes and the potatoes 1 hour. As each vegetable cooks, remove the parcel and wrap in an extra layer of foil to keep warm. Set aside. Shortly before serving, loosen the tops of all the parcels, except the garlic, and put them all back on the coals so the vegetables dry out a little before serving.

Meanwhile, make the tomato salsa. Put a lightly oiled grill rack in place to heat. Sprinkle the tomatoes with sugar, chilli flakes and seasoning. Place them on the grill rack above the vegetables and cook, covered, for 5 minutes. Drain the hickory chips and place a small handful on the coals, replace the cover and leave to smoke for a further 5 minutes. Add some more wood chips and grill for 10 minutes more, or until the tomatoes have dried a little. Remove the tomatoes from the rack and spoon the flesh from the charred skins into a bowl, crush with a fork and mix in the other ingredients. Serve with the vegetables.

The vegetables taste wonderful with grilled marinated sirloin steaks, or with Parmesan cheese shaved on top.

belmont sausage
with mushroom relish

Serves 6–8

450g/1lb skinless and boneless belly pork, cut into large pieces

450g/1lb pork shoulder, cut into large pieces

300–400g/11–14oz back fat, cut into large pieces

50g/2oz/1 cup freshly made breadcrumbs

2 garlic cloves, chopped

10ml/2 tsp salt

10ml/2 tsp ground coriander

5ml/1 tsp ground black pepper

5ml/1 tsp ground cumin

1.5ml/¼ tsp cayenne pepper

1.5ml/¼ tsp ground cinnamon

45ml/3 tbsp chopped fresh basil

60ml/4 tbsp chopped fresh marjoram

60ml/4 tbsp chopped fresh flat leaf parsley

enough cleaned sausage casings for just over 900g/2lb sausage: about 50g/2oz or 2.7m/9 feet

30ml/2 tbsp olive oil for brushing

6 metal skewers

For the relish

45ml/3 tbsp extra virgin olive oil

2 onions, finely chopped

2 garlic cloves, finely chopped

150g/5oz/2 cups chestnut mushrooms, finely chopped

25g/1oz/3 tbsp drained sun-dried tomatoes in oil, finely chopped

90ml/6 tbsp water

20ml/4 tsp sugar

30ml/2 tbsp chopped fresh flat leaf parsley

30ml/2 tbsp sherry vinegar

salt and ground black pepper

I used to make this sausage with the children at the infant school my sons attended. They all loved the process of making sausages from scratch and got the hang of it very quickly, screaming and giggling as the first sausage was filled. The recipe changes every time I get the mincer out, so the Belmont Sausage, named after the school, lives up to its namesake as a learning experience. This time it is a long, traditional Cumberland shape curled into a round.

Pass both meats through the mincer (grinder) once and the back fat twice, using the plate with the widest holes. Place in a large bowl and add the breadcrumbs. Crush the chopped garlic to a paste with a pinch of the salt, then add to the meats with the remaining sausage ingredients except the remaining salt, the casings and the oil. Mix thoroughly with clean hands. Cover and chill overnight.

Rinse the casing by running cold water through it. The easiest way to do this is to fit one end on to the tap (faucet). Just make sure the other end is in the sink, or you could be drenched. Remove the plate with the holes from the mincer and fit the casing on to the sausage-making attachment. If you haven't got one of these you can improvise with a trimmed-to-size plastic funnel that fits on the end or even use a piping bag with a wide nozzle. Add the remaining salt to the mixture and mix well. Fill the casing in one continuous length, leaving a gap of 13cm/5in of empty casing halfway, then separate into two sausages, securing each by tying the ends. Curl each sausage into a round, cover and chill until ready to use.

Make the relish. Heat the oil in a pan and fry the onions and garlic for about 10 minutes until soft and golden. Add the mushrooms and sun-dried tomatoes and fry for 1 minute. Stir in the water and boil until it has evaporated. Stir in the sugar, parsley and sherry vinegar. Season well with salt and black pepper, cover and cool before use.

Prepare the barbecue. Skewer the sausages to maintain the round shape. Once the flames have died down, rake the hot coals to one side and insert a drip tray flat beside them. Position a lightly oiled grill rack over the coals to heat. When the coals are medium-hot, or covered with a moderate coating of ash, brush the sausages with a little oil and place them on the grill rack over the drip tray. Cover with a lid or tented heavy-duty foil, and cook for 5–7 minutes on each side, or until cooked and golden. Serve with the relish, and the juices from the drip tray, if you wish.

lamb mechoui
with cumin and sea salt

This Moroccan speciality often consists of a whole lamb grilled slowly over a charcoal fire for many hours. This version is a large shoulder, rubbed with spices and chargrilled. When cooked, the meat is hacked off and dipped in roasted salt and cumin. The best barbecue for this is the sort that swings into an upright position so the red-hot coals are vertical, with the spit rotating in front of them. Other barbecues will also work but use a lid to ensure slow, even cooking.

Serves 4–6

1 shoulder of lamb, about 1.8kg/4lb

4 garlic cloves, crushed

15ml/1 tbsp paprika

15ml/1 tbsp freshly ground cumin seeds

105ml/7 tbsp extra virgin olive oil

45–60ml/3–4 tbsp finely chopped mint leaves

a few sturdy thyme branches, for basting

salt and ground black pepper

To serve

45ml/3 tbsp cumin seeds

25ml/1½ tbsp coarse sea salt

Open up the natural pockets in the lamb, and stuff with the garlic cloves. Mix the paprika, ground cumin and seasoning and rub all over the shoulder. Cover and leave the lamb for about 1 hour. Mix the oil and mint in a bowl for basting the meat during roasting.

Prepare a barbecue. Once the flames have died down, rake the hot coals to one side and insert a drip tray flat beside them. Position a lightly oiled grill rack over the coals to heat. When the coals are medium-hot, or covered with a moderate coating of ash, place the lamb shoulder on the grill rack over the drip tray covered with a lid or tented heavy-duty foil. For the initial 30 minutes turn the meat frequently, basting using the thyme branches and mint oil. Roast for a further 2 hours, turning and basting every 15 minutes. If you need to replenish the coals, do so before the heat is too low. It will take about 10 minutes to heat sufficiently to continue the cooking.

Dry-roast the cumin seeds and coarse salt for 2 minutes in a heavy frying pan. Do not let them burn. Tip them into a mortar and pound with the pestle until roughly ground.

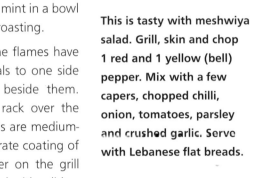

This is tasty with meshwiya salad. Grill, skin and chop 1 red and 1 yellow (bell) pepper. Mix with a few capers, chopped chilli, onion, tomatoes, parsley and crushed garlic. Serve with Lebanese flat breads.

When the meat is cooked, remove from the barbecue, wrap in double foil and rest it for 15 minutes. Serve sliced with the roasted cumin and salt for dipping.

barbecue roast beef
with chimay and horseradish mop

Mopping is big in the Southwestern states of the USA, where the technique is often used to keep large pieces of meat, like whole hog roasts, moist and succulent during the long, slow cooking process. For this recipe, the technique is adapted. No mop is used at the start, so that the meat acquires a healthy glow. It is then mopped constantly, a task best performed by someone who enjoys quiet contemplation with a glass of something refreshing close at hand.

Serves 4

800g/1¾lb beef fillet (tenderloin)

30ml/2 tbsp bottled grated horseradish

30ml/2 tbsp olive oil

120ml/4fl oz/½ cup Chimay

salt and ground black pepper

Pat the beef dry with kitchen paper and place it in a dish. Rub it all over with 5ml/1 tsp of the horseradish and the olive oil. Cover and leave to marinate for 2 hours in a cool place.

If spit roasting, skewer the meat with a long spit. Prepare the barbecue. Mix the remaining horseradish with the beer in a deep bowl. Season the meat well. Once the flames have died down, position a lightly oiled grill rack over the coals to heat. When the coals are very hot, or with a light coating of ash, cook the beef for about 2 minutes on each side, so that the outside sears and acquires a good colour.

Chimay is a naturally brewed beer from Belgium, which could be substituted with any other good-quality beer you fancy. Non-alcoholic beers are also fine, or even soda water, if you want.

Set the spit turning over the coals. Dip a large basting brush in the horseradish and beer mixture and generously mop the meat all over with it. Continue to mop, as the meat turns, for a total grilling time of 11 minutes. Use all the basting mixture. If cooking the meat over a normal grill rack, simply turn and mop the meat frequently.

Rest the meat under tented foil for about 10 minutes before slicing thickly. This dish is great served hot, with roasted vegetables, or left to go cold and eaten with thick slices of country-style bread and horseradish-flavoured mayonnaise.

smoked chicken
with roasted butternut pesto

Serves 4–6

1.3kg/3lb roasting chicken

1 lemon, quartered

8–10 fresh bay leaves

3 branches fresh rosemary

15ml/1 tbsp olive oil

salt and ground
black pepper

kitchen string (twine)

4 handfuls hickory wood
chips soaked in cold water
for at least 30 minutes

For the pesto

1 butternut squash,
about 675g/1½lb, halved
and seeded

2 garlic cloves, sliced

2 fresh thyme sprigs

45ml/3 tbsp olive oil

25g/1oz/⅓ cup freshly grated
Parmesan cheese

Whole chicken smoked over hickory wood chips acquires a perfectly tanned skin and succulent pinkish flesh. The butternut squash roasts alongside it, wrapped in foil, and is later transformed into a delicious pesto. The chicken also tastes great cold so, if your barbecue is large enough, try smoking two at once, for a delicious meal the next day.

Prepare the barbecue. Cut away any excess fat from the opening to the chicken cavity, season the inside and stuff with lemon quarters, bay leaves and sprigs from one rosemary branch. Tie the legs together with kitchen string (twine) and rub the bird all over with the oil. Season the skin lightly.

Prepare the butternut squash for the pesto. Cut it into eight pieces and lay them on a piece of double foil. Season well and scatter with the garlic and thyme leaves. Drizzle over 15ml/1 tbsp of the olive oil and a sprinkling of water. Bring the sides of the foil up to completely enclose the squash and secure the parcel.

Once the flames have died down, rake the hot coals to one side and insert a drip tray beside them. Fill the drip tray with water. Position a lightly oiled grill rack over the coals to heat. When the coals are hot, or covered with a light coating of ash, place the chicken on the grill rack above the drip tray, with the squash next to it, over the coals. Cover with a lid or tented heavy-duty foil. Cook the squash for 35 minutes, or until tender.

Drain the hickory chips and carefully add a handful to the coals, and replace the lid. Cook the chicken for 1–1¼ hours more, adding a handful of hickory chips every 15 minutes. Add the remaining rosemary to the coals with the last batch of hickory chips. When the chicken is done, transfer it to a plate, cover with tented foil and leave to stand for 10 minutes.

In small barbecues, the coals may need to be replenished during cooking. Lift off the rack and chicken before the heat is too low and re-fuel. The coals will take about 10 minutes to heat sufficiently to continue. Allow for this in your timing calculations.

Unwrap the butternut squash. Leaving the thyme stalk behind, scoop the flesh and the garlic into a food processor. Pulse until the mixture forms a thick purée. Add the Parmesan, then the remaining oil, pulsing to ensure it is well combined. Spoon into a bowl and serve with the hot chicken. If the chicken is to be eaten cold, cover it once it has cooled.

spatchcocked quail
with couscous stuffing

These delicate baby birds can be cooked very efficiently on a kettle barbecue with a lid. If your barbecue doesn't have its own lid, improvise with a large upturned wok with a wooden handle – and discover the satisfaction of using an improvised tool that actually works. Serve with a salad of halved cherry tomatoes soaked in really good olive oil, seasoned and scattered with plenty of fresh basil.

Serves 8

8 quail

400ml/14fl oz/1⅔ cups water

2 lemons

60ml/4 tbsp extra virgin olive oil

45ml/3 tbsp fresh tarragon leaves

125g/4¼oz/generous ⅔ cup couscous

15g/½oz dried (bell) peppers, finely chopped

8 black olives, pitted and chopped

salt and ground black pepper

16 wooden or metal skewers

Cut the backbones away from each quail and place them in a pan. Add the water and bring to the boil, then simmer gently to reduce the liquid by half. While the stock is cooking, wipe the insides of each bird with kitchen paper. If you find a heart inside, add it to the stock pot. Place each quail in turn breast uppermost on a board, and flatten it by pressing firmly on the breastbone. Carefully loosen the quail skin over the breasts with your finger, creating a pocket for stuffing later.

Grate the rind from the lemons. Set half the rind aside and put the rest in a flat dish. Squeeze both lemons and add the juice to the dish with 30ml/ 2 tbsp of the oil and 15ml/1 tbsp of the chopped tarragon. Add the quail, turn to coat them well, cover and leave to marinate while you prepare the couscous stuffing.

Place the couscous in a medium bowl and add the chopped dried peppers and seasoning. The stock should have reduced considerably by now. Strain 200ml/7fl oz/scant 1 cup over the couscous, cover with a dry cloth and leave to stand for 10 minutes.

Mix in the reserved lemon rind with the olives and the remaining tarragon and oil. Spread the mixture on a plate to cool, then cover and chill. When cold, ease a little stuffing into the breast pocket on each quail. If using wooden skewers, soak them in cold water for 30 minutes.

Prepare the barbecue. Pin the legs and wings of each quail to the body by driving a long skewer right through from either side to form a cross. If you want, wrap the leg tips with foil to prevent them from getting too charred.

A lid is important for these fragile quail as it is best not to turn them. When enclosed, the heat circulates around the food, cooking it on all sides.

Once the flames have died down, position a lightly oiled grill rack over the coals to heat. When the coals are medium-hot, or with a moderate coating of ash, place the spatchcocked quail on the grill rack and cook for about 5 minutes, moving the birds around occasionally. Cover with a lid or tented heavy-duty foil and cook for 10 minutes. If they are plump and nicely browned they will almost certainly be done. If not, give them a further 5 minutes. Let them stand for a few minutes to cool a little, as they are best eaten with fingers.

Serves 6

6 sea trout cutlets, about 115g/4oz each, or wild or farmed salmon

2 garlic cloves, chopped

1 fresh long red chilli, seeded and chopped

45ml/3 tbsp chopped Thai basil

15ml/1 tbsp palm sugar or granulated sugar

3 limes

400ml/14fl oz/1⅔ cups coconut milk

15ml/1 tbsp Thai fish sauce

thai marinated sea trout

Sea trout has a superb texture and a flavour like that of wild salmon. It's best served with strong but complementary flavours such as chillies and lime that cut the richness of the flesh.

Place the sea trout cutlets in a shallow dish. Using a pestle, pound the garlic and chilli in a large mortar to break it up roughly. Add 30ml/2 tbsp of the Thai basil with the sugar and continue to pound to a rough paste. Grate the rind from 1 lime and squeeze it. Mix the rind and juice to the chilli paste, with the coconut milk. Pour the mixture over the cutlets, cover and chill the mixture for about 1 hour. Cut the remaining limes into wedges.

Remove the fish from the refrigerator so that it can return to room temperature. Prepare the barbecue. Once the flames have died down, position a lightly oiled grill rack over the coals to heat. When the coals are cool to medium-hot, or with a thick to moderate coating of ash, remove the cutlets from the marinade. Place them in an oiled hinged wire fish basket or directly on the grill rack. Cook the fish for 4 minutes on each side, trying not to move them. They may stick to the grill rack if not seared first.

Strain the remaining marinade into a pan, reserving the contents of the sieve. Bring the marinade to the boil, simmer gently for 5 minutes, then stir in the contents of the sieve and continue to simmer for 1 minute more. Add the Thai fish sauce and the remaining Thai basil. Lift each fish cutlet on to a plate, pour over the sauce and serve with the lime wedges.

prawns wrapped in pandanus leaf

These huge prawns can grow up to 33cm/13in in length, and are perfect for grilling on a barbecue. This dish is fast and easy, yet impressive; ideal for a relaxed poolside lunch with salad or for serving as an appetizer while the main course is cooking.

Serves 6

6 giant Mediterranean prawns (extra large jumbo shrimp), total weight about 900g/2lb

juice of 2 limes

60ml/4 tbsp olive oil

12 large kaffir lime leaves

12 pandanus leaves

6 wooden cocktail sticks (toothpicks)

2 limes cut into wedges, to serve

Soak the cocktail sticks in water for 30 minutes. Make a shallow cut down the curved back of each prawn. Put the prawns into a shallow dish. In a separate bowl, mix the lime juice and oil together and pour over the prawns. Set aside for 15 minutes. Take each prawn, lay two kaffir lime leaves on top, wrap two pandanus leaves around it and skewer with a cocktail stick.

Prepare the barbecue. Once the flames have died down, position a lightly oiled grill rack over the coals to heat. When the coals are medium-hot, or with a moderate coating of ash, grill the wrapped prawns for 3 minutes on each side. Serve with lime wedges. To eat, unwrap the prawns, peel off the shell and remove the black vein with your fingers.

Serve these with a really easy dip made by mixing together 150ml/¼ pint/ ⅔ cup mayonnaise and 20ml/4 tsp Thai sweet chilli sauce.

cockle and seafood bake

A beach bake is a semi-precise science and requires a generous pinch of defiant commitment by at least two highly motivated parties with a penchant for digging holes. That said, cooking on a beach is always great fun, and waiting for the seafood to cook is a wonderful way of honing the appetite. Provide lemons, plenty of long thin sticks of bread, really good olive oil for dipping and plenty of wine.

**Approximate quantities
for each person**

2 freshwater crayfish

4 langoustines

**2 large clams, about
6cm/2½in across**

6 small clams

3 whelks

12 cockles

**lemons, bread and good
quality olive oil**

**Other things
you will need**

sand or earth

shovels and buckets

dry pebbles

**plenty of dry firewood,
newspaper and twigs**

matches or a lighter

long-handled rake

**seaweed, well washed and
soaked in water**

**a large piece of canvas,
soaked in water**

12 heavy stones

heatproof gloves

cocktail sticks (toothpicks)

Dig a pit at least 90cm/3ft square x 30cm/1ft deep; larger if you are catering for a crowd. Line the base with pebbles, taking them part of the way up the sides. Build a pyramid-shaped mound of kindling in the middle of the square, with some scrunched-up newspaper at the base. Start the fire. When the wood is burning well add larger pieces to the fire so that it eventually covers the entire surface area of the pit. Keep the fire well stoked up for about 45–60 minutes, then let it burn down to a stage where small glowing embers remain. Using a long-handled rake, pull as many of the dying embers as possible from the pit without dislodging the pebbles. Douse the discarded embers with water to avoid fire-walking incidents.

At this point it is important to retain the oven-like temperature of the pebbles so, working quickly, spread half the seaweed evenly over the pebbles. Arrange the seafood over the seaweed, with the smallest items towards the edges for easy access, as these will cook first. Cover with the rest of the seaweed, then cover the lot with the wet canvas. This should extend beyond the perimeter of the pit and should be weighted down with 12 heavy stones, placed well away from the pit.

The hotter the pebbles get, the faster the food will cook. Do check the smaller items after one hour to see if they are ready.

Leave the seafood to bake undisturbed for 1–2 hours. After 1 hour, have a sneaky peek to see if the cockles and small clams are cooked. These can be taken out at this stage and eaten, and the rest of the seafood enjoyed when it is ready.

grilled lobster
with basil mayonnaise

This is a smart yet unpretentious dish and well worth the little bit of extra effort. Lobster is a fantastic ingredient to cook with but, being a bit squeamish, I find dispatching it a very hard thing to do without giving way to a bit of nervous laughter. This is a job best left to the fishmonger.

To make the basil oil, place the basil leaves in a bowl and pour boiling water over them. Leave for about 30 seconds until the leaves turn a brighter green. Drain, refresh under cold running water, drain again, then squeeze dry in kitchen paper. Place in a food processor. Add both oils and process to a purée. Scrape into a bowl, cover and chill overnight.

Serves 2–4

15 fresh basil leaves, roughly chopped

60ml/4 tbsp olive oil

1 garlic clove, crushed

2 freshly killed lobsters, cut in half lengthways and cleaned

salt and ground black pepper

2 limes, halved, to serve

For the basil oil and mayonnaise

40g/1½oz/1½ cups basil leaves stripped from their stalks

175ml/6fl oz/¾ cup sunflower oil, plus extra if needed

45ml/3 tbsp olive oil

1 small garlic clove, crushed

2.5ml/½ tsp dry English (hot) mustard

10ml/2 tsp lemon juice

2 egg yolks

ground white pepper

Line a sieve with muslin and set it over a deep bowl. Pour in the basil and oil purée and leave undisturbed for about 1 hour, or until all the oil has filtered through into the bowl. The solids left behind in the sieve can now be discarded. Cover well and chill the oil until needed.

To make the mayonnaise, you will need 200ml/7fl oz/scant 1 cup basil oil. If you do not have enough, make it up with more sunflower oil. Place the crushed garlic in a bowl. Add the mustard with 2.5ml/½ tsp of the lemon juice and a little salt and white pepper. Mix well. Whisk in the egg yolks, then start adding the basil oil, a drop at a time, whisking continuously until the mixture starts to thicken. At this stage it is usually safe to start adding the oil a little faster. When you have 45ml/3 tbsp oil left, whisk in the remaining lemon juice and then add the rest of the oil. Finally, whisk in 7.5ml/1½ tsp cold water. Cover the mayonnaise and chill until needed.

If you have to kill the lobster yourself, then do it humanely. Freeze the lobster for 2 hours, then plunge it into a pan of boiling, heavily salted water for 2 minutes. Plunge it into cold water then cut in half. Remove the gritty stomach sac from behind the eyes, the black intestinal canal and gills.

Prepare the barbecue. Chop the basil and mix it with the oil and garlic in a bowl. Season lightly. Once the flames have died down, rake the coals to get more on one side than the other. Position a lightly oiled grill rack over the coals to heat. When the coals are medium to cool, or with a moderate to thick coating of ash, brush some of the oil mixture over the cut side of each lobster half. Place cut-side down on the grill rack on the side away from the bulk of the coals. Grill for 5 minutes. Turn the lobsters over, baste with more oil mixture and cook for 10–15 minutes more, basting and moving about the rack occasionally. Grill the lime halves at the same time, placing them cut-side down for 3 minutes. This helps to release their juices and gives a slight caramel flavour. Serve the lobster with the mayonnaise and the grilled lime halves.

chargrilled pineapple
with pineapple and chilli granita

This is a bold dessert; attractive too, if you leave the green tops on the pineapple. Heating pineapple really brings the flavour to the fore and, with the ice-cold granita, it's the ideal finish to a glamorous barbecue.

Serves 8

2 medium, fresh pineapples

15ml/1 tbsp caster (superfine) sugar

For the granita

15ml/1 tbsp sugar

1 fresh long mild red chilli, seeded and finely chopped

900ml/1½ pints/3¾ cups pineapple juice or fresh purée

To make the granita, place the sugar and chilli in a small heavy pan with 30ml/2 tbsp of the pineapple juice. Heat gently until the sugar has dissolved, then bring to a fast boil for 30 seconds. Pour the remaining pineapple juice into a large, shallow freezerproof container. The ideal size is about 25 x 14cm/10 x 5½in. Stir in the chilli mixture and freeze for 2 hours.

Fork the frozen edges of the sorbet mixture into the centre and freeze for a further 1½ hours until crunchy. Give it another fork over. Return it to the freezer for up to 1 week.

Cut each pineapple lengthways into four equal wedges, slicing right through the leafy crown. Remove the core from each wedge, if it seems tough. Mix the sugar and 15ml/1 tbsp water in a small bowl. Heat the griddle over a high heat, until a drop of water sprinkled on the surface evaporates instantly. Lower the heat slightly. Brush the cut sides of the pineapple wedges with the sugar mixture and grill for about 1 minute on each side, or until branded with grill marks. Serve warm with the granita. If the granita has been in the freezer a long time, thaw for about 10 minutes in the refrigerator before serving and fork it over to break up the ice crystals.

calvados-flamed bananas
with rich butterscotch sauce

My Dutch neighbour gave me this idea. She uses rum and cooks the bananas right in the ashes but they work just as well cooked on the grill rack. It is wise to have a sensible person dealing with the flaming part of this dish, which makes a spectacular end to a meal.

Serves 6

115g/4oz/generous ½ cup sugar

150ml/¼ pint/⅔ cup water

25g/1oz/2 tbsp butter

150ml/¼ pint/⅔ cup double (heavy) cream

6 large slightly underripe bananas

90ml/6 tbsp Calvados

Place the sugar and water in a large pan and heat gently until the sugar has dissolved. Increase the heat and boil until the mixture turns a rich golden caramel colour. Remove from the heat and carefully add the butter and cream; the mixture will foam up in the pan. Replace it over a gentle heat and stir to a smooth sauce, then pour into a bowl. When cool, cover and chill until needed.

Prepare the barbecue. Wrap the bananas individually in foil. Once the flames have died down, position a grill rack over the coals to heat. When the coals are hot, or with a light coating of ash, grill the wrapped bananas for 10 minutes. Remove them to a tray, open up the parcels and slit the upper side of each banana. Gently warm the Calvados in a small pan, then pour some of the Calvados into each banana. Put them back on the barbecue and wait for a few seconds before carefully igniting the Calvados with a long match. Serve the bananas with the chilled sauce as soon as the flames go out.

index

First published by Aquamarine in 2002

© Anness Publishing Limited 2002

Aquamarine is an imprint of
Anness Publishing Limited
Hermes House, 88-89 Blackfriars Road
London SE1 8HA

Published in the USA
by Aquamarine, Anness Publishing Inc.
27 West 20th Street, New York NY 10011
www.lorenzbooks.com

A CIP catalogue for this book is available from the
British Library.

Publisher Joanna Lorenz
Managing editor Linda Fraser
Senior editor Margaret Malone
Design Maggie Town and Beverly Price
Food stylist Linda Tubby
Stylist Helen Trent
Copy editor Jenni Fleetwood
Editorial reader Joy Wotton
Production controller Ann Childers

10 9 8 7 6 5 4 3 2 1

Acknowledgements Special thanks must go to Margaret Malone who,
along with Linda Fraser, gave energy and creative enthusiasm to make
this a treasure of a project. Thanks to Martin Brigdale for such superbly
creative photography, to Helen Trent for consistently wonderful styling.
My husband Jerry, and sons Dan and Ben, for their endless patience when
trying all the dishes and for their enthusiasm when desperate for a joined-
up meal. I'd also like to thank Gustava, Mila and Daniel for insight into
umus and hungies, Paul Gayler for support and advice, Phil and Eddie at
Covent Garden Fisheries for beautiful fish and expert advice, Martin and
John at Panzers for excellent service, Andrew at M & C for vegetable
advice and a warm welcome, Di and Dan at Mortimer and Bennet for help
in all things culinary, Lesley Faddy for her culinary knowledge, Clare Barber
for support, and Ireen for neighbourly advice on flaming bananas.

Publisher's acknowledgements We would like to thank Linda Fraser,
Deirdre Spencer, Martin Brigdale and Helen Trent and for the loan of
their houses for photography.

Publisher's note The reader should not regard the ideas,
recommendations and techniques expressed and described in this book
as substitutes for the advice given in manufacturers' guidelines as to
using a barbecue and any related equipment. Any use to which the
recommendations, ideas and techniques are put is at the reader's sole
discretion and risk.

Suppliers
Equipment
Pizza servers and aluminium trays from Nisbits catering equipment
Telephone 01454 855555
www.nisbits.co.uk

Ingredients
Most ingredients used in the recipes can be found in supermarkets and
good food stores. The following are also available from their suppliers:

Australian aniseed myrtle from Cherikoff, The Rare Spice Company
Telephone 020 7737 3777
E-mail: sales@bespoke-foods.co.uk y

Dried chillies from The Cool Chile Company
Telephone 0870 063 6675
E-mail: orders@coolchile.co.uk

Pandanus and banana leaves, kuchai and all Thai produce from Paya Thai
Telephone 020 8332 2959
www.payathai.co.uk

Notes
Bracketed terms are intended for American readers.
For all recipes, quantities are given in both metric and imperial
measures and, where appropriate, measures are also given in standard
cups and spoons. Follow one set, but not a mixture, because they are
not inter-changeable.
Standard spoon and cup measures are level. 1 tsp = 5ml, 1 tbsp = 15ml,
1 cup = 250ml/8fl oz.
Australian standard tablespoons are 20ml. Australian readers should use
3 tsp in place of 1 tbsp for measuring small quantities of flour, salt, etc.
Medium (US large) eggs are always used unless otherwise stated.